D0001336

One man rearranged me.
One man said write a book.

THE

SECOND

SEDUCTION

FRANCES LEAR

ALFRED A. KNOPF   NEW YORK   1992

FRANCES LEAR

CONTENTS

This book is a granddaughter of *Poor and Proud*, an early-nineteenth-century novel about a girl who got it in the ass at birth and prevailed.

THE
SECOND
SEDUCTION

BIRTH
Hudson, New York, 1923

THE QUESTION IS whether or not Evelyn should have been born at all. Unwanted—by itself reason enough—she was brought to term in the Vanderheusen Home for Wayward Girls in Hudson, a bleak railroad town in upstate New York. Evelyn's mother, unmarried, was scarcely into her teens. The child's father was absent then and forever. Her grandparents hid their shame behind lace curtains in a nearby suburban home. The likelihood is that Evelyn's mother was impregnated during her first psychotic break, transmitting her flawed gene and dark psychology to her unborn child. As fetus, Evelyn was a strong argument for abortion.

The love between mother and child was exchanged only when they were biologically one. (They sent their love for each other into the air for the length of their lives, but it landed elsewhere.) The gestation period completed, Evelyn was orphaned, severed forever from her sole point of connectedness. On July 14, 1923, pre-dawn, her life, not called for, a burden, began.

Evelyn was transferred to an orphanage fifty

miles away where she was parented by a series of hands, abrupt, hurried, on their route to other needy babies in this most transient of nurseries. Evelyn's only sustenance was liquid from a bottle. Her mother, sustained by nothing, mourned in the mothers' wing, locked off from the nursery. All the other women had signed away their babies before giving birth. The separation was irreversible. Not so with Evelyn's mother, who refused to release her child for adoption.

Why not? Was Evelyn's mother intending to retrieve her baby in the future? Was she caught up in some fantasy, the result of her psychosis mixed with depression? Her decision sentenced Evelyn to the orphanage for fourteen months longer than was necessary. She would have been adopted at once. The child was a magnet for love. Within the spare emotional trappings of her institutional home, Evelyn became a permanent receptacle for want.

Evelyn's early life contained a rare absence of grace. She was Satan's bauble. The odds stacked high against her, the question persists: Should she have been born at all?

Her answer? "I would have been better off dead."

Evelyn is me.

FRANCES LOEB

ORPHANAGE

THE BUILDING IS still standing, a discarded, soundless home for children without parents, or children with one parent who could not afford to keep them, or children with two parents who for some reason rejected them and turned them over to the state, or children who had been separated by law from their parents because of ill treatment. Those who had parents, or one parent, could be visited on Sundays. Once in a while, a child was reclaimed by a parent and taken home. All the children were obliged to leave the orphanage on their sixteenth birthday, whether or not they had a place to go. There were no parents visiting in the nursery for the newborns who were up for adoption. The women and men who were childless, or who had children and wanted another, sat in the public rooms Sunday after Sunday looking over the infants, finally choosing one to adopt. The older children were never chosen but lived in the orphanage the length of their childhood.

Herb and Aline Loeb were very particular. They wanted a little girl who resembled them enough to be their own offspring, a child with the same religious background, with educated, healthy parents who would not come after the child at a later date. The Loebs drove to the orphanage four times before they made their selection. My earliest recollection, the most detailed picture I can summon up from my early childhood, is walking around a large building with Aline. She is holding one of my hands, an attendant is holding the other. I recognized the walls of red brick when I returned to find clues to my beginnings in my twenty-second year, when I was living with Phil Smit. He and I drove to Hudson every Sunday for six months, and I played with the children, staring deeply into their eyes to find traces of me as I once was. There was one boy, wiry and rebellious, in whose behavior I found reason, an excuse, for my own.

The grounds had been green and immaculate; now they are covered with debris. There are no doors or windows but for a few that are broken. Six decades ago, the glass in the windows was wiped clean each week. Repairs were made by a small army of men who lived in the town, and the local women serviced the kitchen and cleaned up the rooms. The woman in charge reminded me later of Miss Stewart, my principal in elementary school. Both women wore buns at the back of their heads, no makeup, and the same expression, stern with traces of kindness.

When I was seven years old, I asked Aline why she had chosen me, not another little girl.

"You were the prettiest child in the nursery."

Aline's obsession with appearance taught me that if children were chosen for adoption—perhaps even to love—because they were pretty, then looks were very important in this world. Aline's vanity was her first legacy to me.

A small wooden-framed triptych of me as an infant rests on the table near my bed, and I sometimes look in that tiny child's eyes to see who I was before I became me.

MY ADOPTIVE MOTHER: the one who kept me shut in my room until my bowl-shaped haircut from the orphanage had grown out; the one who would not allow herself to get pregnant lest the pitch of her breasts be lowered; the one who had three abortions after she and my father adopted me; the one with the perfect nose; the one with wit that charmed everyone in her circle in Westchester, New York; the one who kept a high shelf in the closet filled with presents wrapped and marked by sex, by age, by value, so that no one would leave the house empty-handed; the one whose flawless taste influenced my own; the one who wore exquisite lingerie and stylish clothes from Paris and expensive jewelry from my stepfather; the one who would not let me go to my father's funeral; the one who made a play for Jack Schwab after my father died because Mr. Schwab had the most money in her crowd; the one who would not listen to my tales of school or friends or accomplishments or defeats; the one who forbade Bob Goodman, my first love, to see me again after she had the maid spy on us and Bob had kissed my naked breast; the one who walked quietly into her bedroom and closed the door the night I faced her and my stepfather with the truth about his nightly visits to me; the one who wanted me to be like Claire Meier and told me so; the one who came on to my boyfriends; the one who asked me after I returned from my honeymoon if sex was all it was cracked up to be; the one who would not see me after she was operated on twice for cancer because I upset her; the one who left a hundred thousand dollars of my father's money to my stepfather and ten thousand dollars to me for the ten years that I was "good": that one was a bitch.

ALINE FRIEDMAN LOEB was the strongest and most lasting presence in my childhood, though I loved my father and Nanny more. Some of both the bad and the good in Aline is still in me. I benefited from her fine taste, her sense of humor—unexpected in one with such mediocre intelligence—and suffered from her vanity and her terrifying fear of poverty.

Five years before the Great Depression, before our secure suburban life was shattered, Aline sat for a portrait photographer's camera with her six-year-old daughter. She wore ankle-length black lace and the oval diamond pendant she had inherited from her grandmother. My hair was brushed to a shine and I had on white silk socks and Mary Janes and a pale green silk dress from S. Klein. The photographer fussed about, asking Aline to tilt her head this way or that, to fold her hands, to move her feet sideways an inch or two, but Aline had her own sense of composition. She had an inspired eye for design and color and for putting herself in the center of a mother-and-daughter portrait or, for that matter, in the center of everything. I stood beside her with my hand resting on the carved wooden arm of her high-backed needle-point chair.

The portrait was to be a surprise for my father's birthday and it pleased him. When I discovered the picture a half century after it was taken, I thought Aline was pretty and beautifully groomed, but her face, softened by the photographer's lens, was round, almost fat. She looked bovine. Her arms, fully exposed, should have been feminine and sensual, but they were not. Her eyes were small and dark and mean.

In an outtake of the portrait, punched with tiny holes and marked *proof,* was counter-evidence to the claim that cameras do not lie. My adoptive mother was another animal, not a cow, but a hybrid of donkey, songbird, fox, wombat, dove. One view of her was a jungle, the other an elysian field strewn with a silk-satin French evening gown in the softest shade of gray, gathered in gleaming folds from waist to hem; vases crammed with flowers and dinner parties of quail; homemade pudding for Herb and for me; dazzling charm and exquisite manners; an easy wit; perfected skill at teasing men; energy to equal three women her age; and friends by the carload.

Remembered, too, was her obsession with self that left little room for loving me. As much as I hated Aline, I loved her. As much as she rejected me, I wanted to be with her. She repelled and fascinated me. She gave me the laughter I had as a child, including one night in Florida, where we had gone after my father's death, when we sat on the curb outside our apartment and hugged and kissed and cried with laughter and grief. Aline was a storybook of drama and boredom, with a beginning and a middle but without an ending, until my children's children have forgotten me.

23 WENDT AVENUE
Larchmont, New York, 1924–35

THE WHITE CLAPBOARD HOUSE at 23 Wendt Avenue, Larchmont, New York, had black shutters and a front door that looked like patent leather from years of coats of paint. The magnolia tree in the front yard was too grand for our little home. Each spring it was a marvel, bursting into pink-and-white sculpture, its branches spreading a quarter of the way across our property. The front porch, which we never used, was furnished with green wicker. When the wisteria on the trellis came into bloom, I stood for hours beneath the lavender and green-leafed flower ceiling and breathed in the soft aroma.

My father built a second trellis between the back door and the garage and planted it with grapevines. The green and purple clusters were equally sweet. I sucked out the flesh from the skin, spit out the seeds, and swallowed the pulp whole. Once I got stuck all day in the highest branches of the cherry tree in the backyard until my father came home from work and rescued me. My father tended to the rose garden himself. I watched his strong hands work the earth and trim the branches and cut the buds. An asparagus fern patch was wedged into the corner of the garden. The stalks were ugly when they were young but, when open, they spread out like green lace peacock feathers, which Aline cut and mixed with the flowers around the house. Our furniture was ordinary except for a dreadful dining room suite that Aline had inherited from her mother. It was painted a darkish brown that faded to ochre.

Aline put me in the master bedroom, which had a fireplace, but access to the bathroom was off the hall. She and my father had the smaller bedroom with its own bath. In the mornings, when my father opened my door, I knew it was time to go in and watch him shave. He used a straight razor and sharpened it on a long leather strop. The straight razor is all but extinct, yet to my way of thinking, a man is a truer man if he uses one.

Our home was much the same as most middle-class American suburban homes except for the relationships among the people who lived there. Our family did not love the way families are meant to love. In not one of my memories can I find a moment of emotion between my father and Aline. I never saw them kiss. I like to believe my father kissed me a lot. Aline was outwardly affectionate with me for my father's sake, but she did not like me. After we sold the house in the Great Depression, after my father killed himself, the only things of value that remained from the year when Aline and I lived there alone were still growing in the ground.

NANNY

MY NANNY SMELLED of laundry soap and freshly washed hair. She spoke in sounds that were formed by the thick brogue of her homeland. I was her Little Flower, hyperbole for a child who had grown into angular shapes and a quixotic disposition. Nanny functioned outside the normal boundaries for maids and governesses, exercising an unusually strong degree of discipline and affection toward her charge. I have only thin scraps of memory of her, a plain Irishwoman, infinitely brave, with such audacity for a servant that, at times, she seemed to have been a fictional character who lived only in my imagination. But, no, I have letters from her and confirmation from friends who knew the role Nanny played in the war between Aline and me.

It is true that Aline won eventually, that Nanny was stripped of the power that allowed her to interrupt Aline's anger each day as it set out on its journey toward me. My Nanny, strapping, hands red from washing, back stiff from the early proddings of her own mother, would place her muscled Irish body between my mother and me and put her grand Irish heart in front of mine, risking her pittance salary and free bed and board for a little girl whom she adored, who was not hers now and would not be hers, as it turned out, past the child's seventh year.

Children of unloving mothers who are fortunate to have domestics who love them, escape the fate of becoming their mothers and begetting yet other generations of nonmaternal women who were best left childless. Underneath my mother's loveless treatment of me was her instinctive knowledge that she could not love a child, that she could not understand or feel maternal love. Because my father insisted, they tried to conceive for eight years, but Aline's determination not to become pregnant was greater than the eagerness of Herb's sperm. After I was adopted, her determination lessened. Now she was free to abort her pregnancies since Herb's wish to have a child had been filled.

Aline dreaded the responsibility for me if the Irishwoman left, but leave Nanny did, returning to her beloved Dublin, where she found a good and handsome man with a brogue like hers whom she married. I received many letters from Nanny through the years, written on eggshell-blue airmail stationery, and although I did not answer them regularly, they prompted a feeling in me each time one came and kept my love for her alive, kept it working. Maternal love, as I learned it from Nanny, may be the best part of me.

Nanny taught me, by example, that regular features, prettiness, in a woman's face do not always matter when there is romance between a woman and a man. The good great soul that erupted in Nanny's smile made her truly more beautiful by all the miles of the earth than my mother, who was well known for her good looks. More than a half century after Nanny went back home to find her man to love, I can still summon up, re-experience, the wonder of her unconditional acceptance of me. Her memory still makes me feel like a child who believes she is a fine child, blossoming into a woman, well nurtured by a maternal heart.

A small storage closet under the stairs sheltered me from Aline's anger, which often came on Thursdays and every other Sunday, Nanny's days off. But I remember a Wednesday, ironing day, when Nanny was busy in the basement. No doubt the reason for Aline's most recent scolding was of little consequence since, at the age of five, I committed only minor crimes. Again I was spanked, yelled at, threatened, humiliated, frightened, and, again, I ran to Nanny for comfort. She was halfway up the stairs to the kitchen, having finished her ironing, her arms full of Herb's shirts and my dresses and linen for the table. I remember Nanny's face, crimson red with anger. She knew immediately what had happened. "No wonner she dunna onnerstand yeh. Yeh airn't hair reel choild." There on the middle step of the stairs, my Nanny, who would put her life between me and suffering, told me, not knowing the consequences, that I was adopted. On that day, I became an outsider.

I HAD ONE FRIEND in elementary school. Her name was Janet Greenbaum and she was the tallest girl in my class. Janet had an older brother who was as handsome as she was plain. She and I would watch him play with his friends in the Greenbaums' back-yard after school. Quite by accident one day, without intention, he shot me in the leg with a BB gun as I stood with Janet, partly hidden behind a bush. As was my wont, I took it personally. I took everything personally that happened in my neighborhood, in school, and in any other place I visited. My dislike of myself was full blown when I went to Chatsworth Avenue School, and it blotted out the trusting part of me that Nanny had nurtured.

Aline's constant criticism of the way I looked and behaved was far more powerful in shaping my view of myself than Nanny's admiration. The infant cho-sen for her prettiness changed quickly into a child whose appearance was not altogether pleasing. Cer-tainly not to Aline, whose standards for beauty, es-pecially in a child of hers, were much higher than my looks could ever reach. She complained about my forehead, which was too large and round, and my nose, which was not pert and small as she would have wished. I was a hostile child, angry at her anger at me, a loner soon after I entered school. I was taller than most girls my age, the tallest in my class except for Janet Greenbaum. Aline considered my height unfeminine and was convinced, long before my puberty, that no man would want to marry me. Defeated before my life had begun, I became sullen and disobedient. The other children on my block believed that I was sickly since Aline made me go to bed in daylight when they were still playing—was it stickball?—in the street. I was in perfect health, strong and willful. I turned my strength inward and firmly implanted Aline's disappointed view of me. I was to have been as she was, popular, pretty, attractive to men; instead I did not grow up gracefully, and I was shunned by other children.

The girls who were the most sought after seemed to excel in everything: in their studies, in sports, in after-school activities, even in their dress. Three such girls—Virginia, Barbara, and Doric—had a great influence on my life, for they made me understand that, if I was to succeed in life, I would have to develop some expertise of my own.

Straight-A students Virginia Adler and Barbara Bevin were beautiful, and everybody said that Virginia was rich. Like most popular girls, they had straight, shiny, well-brushed golden-blond hair. All the boys had a crush on one or both of them, leaving the rest of us with long-remembered feelings of inferiority. Doric Alling was to be the most popular girl at Hessian Hills School, and although her hair was light brown, it was well brushed and shiny and straight. Doric drew horses' heads, good ones, from morning to night, and she herself was as graceful as a thoroughbred. She was neither too tall nor too short but the perfect height for dancing with most twelve-year-old boys. I met Doric many years later in the ladies' room at Yankee Stadium and was not unhappy to see that she had become dowdy.

Virginia and Barbara always sat together in the seats at the end of the front row, closest to the window, their hair swaying back and forth like watchmen's lanterns. I spent most of the hours in the school day staring at them, envying their beauty, their perfect noses, their perfect skin, their perfectly formed bodies. Virginia wore embroidered white blouses that made her look very feminine. Barbara was larger, less delicate than Virginia, with a strongly colored, severely tailored style all her own. Physically they were opposites, yet there was, in the two of them, an inner similarity that the other girls did not have.

Answering in class was a rote procedure, the everyday, the usual. Life did not stop when a student rose to recite. There was no great rush of interest, no hush of the class to listen to a child who had learned his or her lessons well. Except when Virginia or Barbara was called on. Then there was a roar of preparation in the room, desks were slammed shut, the entire class leaned forward in their seats, eager to be enchanted by these superior girls who were not just pretty faces but bright and poised and born performers. They earned their popularity. I would have to earn mine.

As a child, I was in awe of writers. I collected photographs of the great writers of the time, who were almost all men. Thus began my secret want. I would be a man and write fine books and be photographed and respected. Neither of my parents liked to read. I was not exposed to music or painting. We never traveled. Nothing in our home was more artistic than a good chocolate cake. Yet I loved people who were sensitive to happenings around them, who made up stories in their imaginations, who wrote poetry that made you cry or laugh. A distant cousin was an editor on a small-town paper, and I marveled at his talent. It seemed to me that the most interesting people on earth were writers. I would, someday, be one too.

To compete successfully in a world full of long-haired blondes with brains, as well as other assorted challenges that popped out at me as I grew older, I isolated a talent in high school and developed a minor skill. I appointed myself the editor of my high school yearbook and wrote it myself, including the class prophecies in which I named myself the first woman editor of *The New York Times.* I had, I thought, the temperament to be a writer. I had been born with the sensitivity, and I had felt the pain.

Chatsworth Avenue Elementary School was located at the bottom of a small hill that began its downward slope at the east end of our property. The hill was just steep enough to keep our sleds going in the icy snow a few yards into the schoolyard. When I revisited 23 Wendt Avenue many years later, the hill was exactly as I remembered although the house was much smaller—as everyone, when grown, sees a childhood home. The school was still there, a little shabbier perhaps. Was that my principal, Miss Stewart, in one of her ankle-length dark-blue chiffon dresses, standing in the doorway, greeting each student by name?

I ALWAYS HAVE an "exitline." A stash of lithium. A building tall enough to kill, not maim, for godsake no, not maim. One goes out in suicide, one simply goes out, gets out, wriggles, bolts, and does not come back merely smashed up or, as the first priority, left with the ability to feel. One does not go out in a half-assed manner. Suicide has many consequences. It will hurt people who love you, it can splatter the side-walks; but its purpose, the reason for its magnetism, is that it is the only guaranteed, surefire way to end, blitz, detonate a critical mass of suffering. Suicide, reduced to its pure essence, is a delivery system that moves us from pain to the absence of pain. If the gods contrive against us and the planets are in disarray, if the earth cracks open beneath us, we must always have a way out.

Suicide nested in my adoptive father's story. His name was Herbert Adam Loeb and he was handsome and tall and he could do anything. He took our fine old gray Packard automobile apart every Saturday and put it back together every Sunday, and he fixed the neighbor's furnace, and he trimmed the privet hedge around our house with immaculate precision.

Each year he pruned the fruit trees and tied back the wisteria vines and covered the rosebushes with burlap. He held me on his lap but seemed not to listen to me as I told him about the days of my young life. My father was a quiet man, withdrawn, and often impatient with me. Many years after his death in my tenth year, in 1933, in the depth of the Great Depression, I understood that Herb was a depressive and could not work out the problems that came to most men during that time.

My father designed his exitline with artistry. His suicide was clean and masterful and seemed not to contain conflict. He shut the doors and windows of the garage, started the car engine, connected a hose to the exhaust pipe, placed the free end next to his face, breathing his death into himself, and did not vomit up pills or crash into someone's terrace awning or lie, a mass of jelly, on the sidewalk. My father was a generous man. He died on the path between the garage and our house where the rescue squad had carried him, his body and face unmarred, still beautiful, although, I noticed, unusually pink.

My father did not recover from his death. He did not return to me. The loss of him cracked apart my life, my heart, the sky above me, the earth beneath my feet. Herb Loeb taught me that the solution to an unsolvable problem is death by one's own hand. As a young woman, I played my own exitlines gingerly lest they be written in cement.

HERB HAD NOT botched the job. Aline returned from the hospital a widow, accompanied by her lawyer, Ira Hirschfeld, and Jack Schwab, a family friend, both of whom she later tried to seduce and marry. A man in a tweed suit whom I did not know held me on his lap and told me that my father was dead. I watched the tears form into huge beads behind his thick glasses and wondered who he was and why a stranger was holding me at a time like this.

Aline passed by without noticing me and went upstairs to her room to change into all black and begin the year-long period of mourning. Aline would go to temple every Friday night for twelve months, dragging me with her, pulling me up to stand beside her to be stared at when it was time for the mourners to rise.

Rabbi Bender was already at the house when Aline arrived. She saw him alone first, before seeing anyone else, before her brother, before me. They were together for over an hour. When he left, I was summoned. I entered the room in which Aline would now sleep alone. She had been crying, her face was clean of makeup. Without embracing me, she pointed to the seat on the couch next to her.

"I can't live without your father, but I'll see to it that you're taken care of."

I took Aline's words literally. I believed that she would die. How could I survive losing both parents in one day?

"You're too young to go to the funeral. I'm sending you to the Meiers'."

I could not go to Herb's funeral? I had more right than anyone to be there. What had I done to be punished this way? I listened to her talk, not hearing what she said, my anger building. There must be a reason for so cruel an announcement. Then, from my instinctive understanding of Aline, from my life's experience with her, I knew, beneath my frustration and tears of rage, that Aline would live. I was not too young to go to the funeral. I was too much a tragic figure—a ten-year-old without a father—too much a threat to Aline's role as principal mourner. I would go to the Meiers', and there would be no child at the funeral to compete with Aline as she stood center stage with her plain black dress and her long veil covering her pretty face.

The Meiers were nice people. The funeral was discussed at the dinner table and I was not surprised to hear that my mother looked lovely but pale, that she stumbled as she entered the little chapel in the funeral home, and that Ira Hirschfeld and Jack Schwab supported her until she sat down. I could have written the scene myself, as well as the little drama at the graveside. I am sure she broke down as the casket was being lowered, wailing some words to the effect that she wanted to be buried with him, that there was no life for her without him.

A month later, Aline took me to the cemetery and stood at one end of the plot and cried, while I stood six feet away from her beside Herb's ivy-covered grave and did not cry. I did not grieve for my father. Children who do not mourn their parents often become depressives. The demon in the adult lives of emotionally damaged children is the unresolved pain of loss, rejection, or abuse. The most difficult behavior to make comprehensible, to budge from its hiding place in the emotional self, is the unending, uncontrollable attraction to revisit the site of the original blow. There is a degree of self-destructiveness in almost everyone.

I gave much weight to Aline's explanation for my father's suicide. Hiding on the staircase when his will was being read, I listened to her blame me for his death. "Herb died because he didn't have enough money to pay Frances's hospital bills. He knew his life insurance would cover the cost of her appendectomy."

My father did commit suicide on the day he brought me home from the hospital after paying the bill, but his business was bankrupt and the bank was ogling the house. There was every reason to believe he had run out of money that day or would the next day or another day soon in the future. Herb had bought his life insurance three months before my appendectomy, and he must have begun to plan his suicide months before that. A man like Herb Loeb does not kill himself on the spur of the moment, yet I believed that Aline spoke the truth.

My father, who looked as solid as the Morgan Bank, was wiped out in 1933 when President Roosevelt gave Americans ten cents for every dollar of their savings. Our entire worth was on deposit in the Larchmont Savings Bank. The town lined up along the sidewalks on the four corners of Larchmont Avenue and stared at the chains pulled across the doors of the town's two banks.

My father's double-indemnity life insurance policy was airtight. A man from the Connecticut Life Insurance Company, which carried my father's policy, explained some forty years later that men contemplating suicide during the Great Depression had taken out large insurance policies, waited a month or two for the policies to be processed, and then killed themselves. The policies were honored if the family could prove accidental death. Aline's lawyer saw to that. The hose that Herb had used was disposed of immediately. There were no witnesses.

Aline collected $300,000, most of which was

spent on herself and her cancer treatments; the rest was left to her next husband. On her death, she sent me a letter. "You were a pleasure to me for ten years, so I am leaving you $10,000. After that you were nothing but trouble."

She was right. After Herb died, my behavior became a revenge at the world, at Aline, at my father for leaving me when I needed him. I am, still, at times, a vengeful woman and, to an extent, a sexist, for I resent the power men have had over me.

THE HAL CO.

THE HAL CO. was a tiny dot in the busy garment district that was the heart of New York City. HAL was an acronym for Herbert Adam Loeb. His company manufactured nurses' and maids' uniforms and was known for a quality product and dependable service. My father, who did not look like a man in the trade, was of German descent and resembled, but had not as perfect a face as, John Gilbert.

THE HAL CO. did business in a rectangular loft, one third as large as a football field, with a corner walled off into a box-shaped office jammed with papers and office furniture. When I went to visit, I watched the men—only men worked there—roll out huge bolts of white cloth into thick layers on the long cutting tables. When the entire bolt had been laid flat, the men took their electric cutting wheels and followed the patterns my father had made. All the men, including my father, had fingers missing from their hands from the days when there was no guard attached to the front of the blade to protect them. My father could do everything from layering the fabric to designing the patterns to sewing, finishing, packing, wrapping, shipping, billing, and keeping the company books. He was a fine craftsman, and he was a pure entrepreneur. Underneath the layers of my memory, like the layers of cloth on my father's cutting tables, is his unassailable reward, his pride in the fine product of THE HAL CO.

Everyone who knew my father said that he adored me. He called me "Swa," from Françoise, but the name Frances came from his mother, whom he admired and loved. I never knew my paternal grandmother, but I tried to be like my father's image of her.

I recall, as if it were yesterday, Herb seated in the leather chair in the den with the lamp aglow over his left shoulder, statuelike, immobile, deep deep in thought. When I first saw the Lincoln Memorial, it reminded me of Herb except that the expressions of the two men were different. There was the same weariness in both but there was less resolve in my father's face. My father often wore another expression, a quizzical, worrisome look that did not belong on a man as rugged as he. I do not know the thoughts in my father's mind when he decided upon, and then planned, his death but the expression on his face was, I am certain, the one I have just described.

Ordinary things remind me of my father, like chocolate pudding, which he ate almost every night for dinner—I put cream on mine, Herb ate his neat —garages with workbenches strewn with tools and rags covered with grease, Christmas toys he put together for me, working on the car or fixing something in the house or planting in his garden. I spent much of my childhood watching my father do things well.

We lived a ten-minute walk from the station where Herb caught the train to the city. In the evenings, he walked the long block to our house, and I knew his silhouette when it was tiny and far in the distance. I waited for him at the corner and, when he was a short distance from me, I ran to him and he picked me up and held me and kissed me. That is one memory I have of my father touching me with love. Once, when Aline was particularly angry at me, my father came into the bathroom where Nanny was giving me a bath and lifted me out of the tub and slapped my body until it was covered with red welts. I remember the sound of those slaps, of my screaming, of Nanny's protests.

I remember loving my father.

HISTORY AND
REPETITION

MY MATERNAL GRANDFATHER, or great-grandfather, or, as the story sometimes goes, my great-
great-grandfather, Colonel Friedman, who fought
with General Grant in the Civil War, was rich, and
so Aline was rich as a child. When she was in her
early twenties, her father, one of the Colonel's lack-
luster heirs, speculated on worthless oil stocks and
lost the family fortune. From then on, until she died,
there was nothing between my mother and poverty
except a husband.

My father stated in his will that his insurance was
to take care of both Aline and me. Aline married Ben
Landau one year to the day after my father died, and
it was to him that she left most of the money, giving
me the deepest financial knifing of my life.

That is the way economic history was written in
my little family. Men make money, men lose money,
children are defrauded or deprived. I think about
stopping the repetition of economic history as it is
written in wills and as it was controlled by Aline and
her forebears. I tell myself that children are better off
not inheriting anything from their parents, that
money left to heirs is more apt to be pissed away or

siphoned off by strangers than treated with respect and acumen. I think there is wisdom in this reasoning, and I would act upon it with my own children except for the off chance that death is a continuation of life: then I am in deep shit.

NORA ZITLOVSKY
Croton, New York, 1936

CHILDREN FROM BROKEN HOMES lived in Nora's boardinghouse during the school year. Her soft, ample girth, natural beauty, and gentle ways soothed us in the months when we were separated from our parents. One or two of the children had occasional visits from one parent, never two, since either the mothers and fathers were divorced or one parent was dead. Aline and Ben went to Europe or the Orient on business every fall and stayed until late spring. I spent the summers with them, the school year with Nora at Hessian Hills School, and my vacations with Aline's widowed friend, Rhoda Troutfeldt.

I learned to be uncomfortable with almost everything about myself at Hessian Hills, especially my kinky and dark brown hair. Eva, Nora's daughter, had long blond braids that were groomed by Nora early each morning and once again before the evening meal. Eva had a strong, slim body and a horse she was in love with that took up most of her day. The only time any of us ever saw Eva was during meals. All the day and into the early evening, she was cleaning dung out of the stable or riding off into the richly carpeted hills behind the school.

Jed was my favorite student in the school, a reed of a boy who could count to a trillion without stopping and could quote Walt Whitman. My first sexual fantasies were about Sheldon Coons, who was rich and handsome and was later killed in World War II. Billie was a homosexual, the first I ever knew. When he could not go to war, he sat in his house by the great Croton Dam, a pale, smileless young man wrapped in a blanket, mourning Sheldon and the other boys from Croton who were killed or wounded overseas.

Among the girls were Lydia G, who was coarse, big-boned, and stupid, and Lydia B, who made the honor roll every month and who mesmerized me with her precise and graceful penmanship. There was fat Martha, who never spoke to anyone, and Evelyn, the smartest girl in school, whose hair fell in a gentle wave across her forehead. I heard many years later that she became a secretary and married her boss just as she had set out to do. There was Margery, who was a member of a wealthy family from suburban Detroit and was disliked because she was a snob, but Margery was popular with the boys from town and she would tell me how they put their erect penises on her naked thigh but "not inside" her. I learned what nice girls did, and did not do, from this daughter of an automotive king.

Twin girls, very tall and very beautiful with exceptional bodies, rode horses with Eva and visited Sheldon Coons at his home. One twin had blond curly hair and small eyes, the other was dark-haired with eyes of average size. They were my first female sex symbols. The skintight blue jeans they wore to school every day clearly outlined their legs and buttocks and the indentation at their crotches. Primo Carnera, a mountain of a man, a great heavyweight champion, came to the school and fought in a boxing exhibition for a benefit fair. He gave me my first kiss, in the back seat of a teacher's car on the way home. I was very excited, and I fantasized about him for a long time. By chance, years later, I sat opposite him in the dining car of a train on my way to Reno to get my first divorce. He did not recognize me.

My teacher wore sandals and was a Jesus freak and taught us about the brotherhood of man. Not to love your fellow man and woman was a sin at Hessian Hills. We studied Edward Bellamy's *Looking Backward* and saw a great new vision of equality and a way to communicate with each other by means of a giant screen stretched across one wall of our living rooms on which we would see films of events as they were happening. Mr. Bellamy knew a lot about telecommunications but less about economic systems. As recently as Gorbachev, I believed everything I had seen and heard in Hessian Hills School, which was run by Elizabeth Moos, who turned out to have been an important member of the Communist Party. I learned commitment to the improvement of life for everyone, and I was ready, shortly after school began, to do battle for any reform the school endorsed. On May Day, a group of us took the train to New York to march in the parade down Fifth Avenue, and I was convinced that I, Frances Loeb, awkward, a nobody, could make life better for working men and women.

(At Hessian Hills School, I learned that anger could be put to legitimate use. The strong emotion I felt when I was twelve years old, during the march down Fifth Avenue alongside men and women who, I was taught, were being treated unfairly, engaged my passion, diverted much of my anger at the world and at myself, and channeled it into a positive force, into causes that I believed in, worked for, and supported throughout my childhood and my adult life.)

A baseball diamond had been cut out of the field behind the school, and each one of us—both boys and girls—took turns playing every position. When I was catcher and Sheldon Coons was pitching, I could not take my eyes off him, so I did not see the ball coming. It went straight into my mouth and broke my jawbone and knocked out some teeth. After I came home from the hospital, I was kept away from the other children for the rest of the year lest anyone bump me and dislodge the intricate braces. I did my schoolwork in the main room of the boardinghouse and went into my room when the children came back in the late afternoon. Nora was the only person I saw. Nora and Eva, who was almost always in the stable.

One Sunday, when the kids were off to church and Nora had made me porridge, which I love, she sat down with me and began to talk very very quietly, a kind of chant timed to the swaying of her huge body, and I heard word after word of affection and encouragement. By the smooth rush of her words, by some odd ring in her voice, I knew that she was giving me a pitch that she had perfected over the years with hundreds of needy children. Nora's business was making uncomfortable children feel better, but I did not believe a word she said. Either she had used them too often until they had become rote or I was not able to receive anything warm or tender or caring in that year when I stayed in my room and taught myself the habit of withdrawing from the world.

I graduated from high school at the Mary A. Burnham School for Girls, across the street from Smith College. We wore long white dresses and carried white bouquets as if we were brides or initiates. I wore lipstick for the first time that day. Aline and Ben were away.

BOB GOODMAN

MY KNOWLEDGE ABOUT MEN began to form early. I recall my mother and my grandmother whispering to each other, while taking the winter sun in the glass-enclosed sitting room off the porch of our Larchmont home. I heard my father's name spoken —Herb this and Herb that—and some words about Henry, the grandfather who had lost all his money in worthless stocks. Having had three fathers—including the biological one—I, too, had stories to tell, but no man had more to do with the shaping of my life than the teenage son of an insurance salesman who lived on our block. Bob Goodman found the place in my heart that Herb had broken, and, with Aline's help, split it further apart.

Only a few sharply focused images remain from my past, but the memory of the night when Bob unbuttoned my blouse and fondled and kissed my breasts is so vivid, so real, that I believe I can still feel his hands and the soft flesh of his mouth. These were ordinary goings-on between a boy and a girl in that space between childhood and being an adult that holds no evil and is the beginning of expressing sexual love. Aline, who did not approve of either fondling

43

or Bob Goodman, had instructed the maid to stand outside the window of the living room, where Bob and I sat together on the couch, and report everything we did. Aline called Bob's parents and told them Bob was never to see me again.

The termination of adolescent love does not tremble the earth. The skies do not cave in when one teenager is substituted for another in the life of an active young girl or boy. Not so in this story. I took the loss of Bob and attached it to my father and my father before that and I compounded the losses exponentially until all love became loss.

I have loved with everything but trust, an inferior way of loving, but I have tried to be good company for my lovers. I have made them laugh, I have been good to them, and I am a great friend of sex. I have made do with what I was but I was not the real thing. A corner of me was an observer, unloving, alert to signs of impending loss. I tested the permanence of all my relationships with men until they finally failed —or I made them fail—the test.

Z. RITA WATTS
New York, New York, 1939

Z. RITA WATTS was close to perfect. Her psychiatric practice, limited to adolescents, was located in a modestly furnished East Side office. She herself was impeccable in her understated elegant uniform, a long-sleeved tailored wool or linen dress decorated with a precisely placed jewel. There was nothing on Z. Rita's composed face or in her cool eyes that her patients could interpret for their own use.

After years of suffering my erratic behavior from my father's abandonment, Aline, as she had done once before when I was ill with Saint Vitus's dance—the catchall diagnosis for nervous children—turned to the psychiatric community for help. Z. Rita seemed an ideal choice: female and an expert in the problems of adolescence. Her tone and deportment impressed Aline, who felt no need to inquire further about the practitioner's professional competence. Aline left Z. Rita's office confident that her daughter would finally be brought under control. The child's nervousness, her disobedience, and her volatility were becoming intolerable.

I was supposed to see Z. Rita the following

Thursday, a long wait, but her calendar, which lay open on her desk, was booked solid with the names of troubled young people. Aline was anxious for the day to arrive, anticipating an immediate cure. Ben was indifferent, having given up arguing against therapy that, in his mind, was useless. I was ambivalent, eager to talk, to confess my secret, to relieve my guilt, but mistrustful of those who listen.

I visited Z. Rita for only one one-hour consultation, but I felt her to be trustworthy and made her the vehicle through which I unburdened myself of the long history of incest with my stepfather. I told Z. Rita every detail of the evenings Ben and I had spent together over the previous four years, down to his habit of taking off his ring before he fondled me. I told her of my response to him, how good his touch made me feel, how I longed for it each night, and how being with Ben made me feel that he and I were our own little family. I told her about the sensations I felt in my flesh, about the aches I felt inside my body, about the wetness between my legs, about my passion from feeling his fingers there. I told her that these were the happiest moments of the years since my father died. Then, as I dredged up the bottom of my soul, I told her that Ben did not come to my room one night, that he never came back again.

Z. Rita listened, expressionless. I told her that I

was certain that he had found something ugly down there, something that might have smelled, something that disgusted him.

"Dr. Watts, I think it is still there."

Strangely, Z. Rita did nothing to assure me that Ben undoubtedly had left for other reasons, most likely that Aline was becoming suspicious of his behavior with me. I wondered for a long time afterward, as I thought back on that moment, why Z. Rita did not reassure me that there was nothing there at all except the sweetness of my adolescent body. It would have saved me from years of terror and shame.

After our session was over, Z. Rita called my mother and made an appointment for the next day. "Bring Mr. Landau too," she said. In a perfectly designed and executed betrayal, Z. Rita repeated to my parents everything I had told her. That evening, when I returned home, Ben met me at the door with a kitchen knife in his hand. Enraged, screaming, his spit spraying from his swollen and crimson face, he aimed the knife at me.

"Tell her"—he pointed to Aline—"tell her you lied."

I have lied many times in my life, so one might wonder why I did not lie to my mother. Her collusion in the incestuous relationship between her husband and her child would have been lifted if I had said, Yes, I lied, I lied for revenge, I lied out of jealousy, I lied out of boredom, I lied for attention, I lied for the drama of this moment, I lied out of some evil in me, I lied because to lie brings me satisfaction. But I did not lie.

"How," I asked, "could I have made up such a thing?"

Aline turned and left the room and went into her bedroom and closed the door and protected her economic hide and sided with Ben and allowed me to fall through the cracks of her life. I saw my mother twice after that. Once after her first operation for cancer of the breast, and once when she lay dying in a large corner room in New York Hospital. I watched Ben as he took off her diamond wedding ring at the moment of her death and slipped it into his pocket. That gesture held, for me, an ugliness that suited him.

I left home that night after Ben had chased me into my room and buried his knife in the door I had slammed shut. I did not fear for my life, but I understood that all the events prior to this moment belonged to my childhood, that the first part of my life was over. As I packed my clothes and counted out the little money I had, I faced the truth. I was on my own and would have to support myself and be responsible for myself, and there would be no fallback position, no recourse, no Santa Claus, no surprise from on high. I was not afraid. I had been alone before. My destiny was to be alone, of that I was certain, but I did not know on that winter evening, nor did I fully realize until I had lived the largest part of my life, that the only hardship I would not be able to bear was loneliness.

BEN

I HAD GAINED a degree of belonging when Ben began to fool around with me. Our probings of each other's genitals placed me inside a system.

The nature of incest is misunderstood. Almost all sexually aware adults have momentary sexual thoughts about the bodies of children. That is one end of the incest spectrum, natural, benign. The other end of the spectrum is an adult satisfying his or her lust, damaging, betraying the child. Some adults, men and women, who hunger for sex with children, or a particular child, are able, without moral restraint or psychological conflict, simply to take the child's body for his or her use. Unspeakable, unimaginable fantasies in the minds of men and women are indulged with innocent, dependent children.

In between the ends of the incest spectrum are countless degrees of appropriate and inappropriate thoughts and actions, which are harmful only when the perpetrator or the victim is acting or reacting with sexual desire. There is a law not yet written any-where, but needed, about the sexual seduction of the young that would relieve them of all culpability for the act and for their response to it. No amount of thought to the contrary can make wrongful, or con-spiratorial, the child in the crime of incest. Nor can the weight of the universe alter the purity of the child's response in feeling sexual pleasure within the incestuous act.

Ben did not penetrate me with his penis, but he loved touching me, and I was hungry for affection. He was a cruel man and he abused my mother in ways that deeply humiliated her, and he abused me, but his hands opened me up and I shone and burst forth and felt myself to be a person, a person to love, a wanted person. For those of us who do not have selves, our existence is an important point to establish, and it can best be done by allowing another to experience our sex.

Aline lay in bed reading. She knew what was going on as her fifty-six-year-old stingy, paunchy husband perverted my body into a haunted, closed, tormented space.

The line of frigid women and men is long, and the process of applying for treatment is slow. The forms to fill out are stacked on tables, and each person in the line has filled out a number of them. Few people are taken for the preliminary interview, which lasts a long time and is the first in a series before a doctor is seen. Some of us step out of the line without having to wait our turn and without having completed the forms. We have found the antidote to the perpetrator. We are now treatable.

The healing of sexual frigidity in the sexually abused man or woman is accomplished, in the final stages, by men and women who are completely secure in their own sexuality and have the patience and the wisdom not to ask for or demand the orgasm that is stuck in the past. It takes strong caring and persistent fucking to drive out the demon finger or penis or tongue or, as has been reported, beer bottle.

ADOLESCENCE

AFTER ALINE HAD TAKEN AWAY the only love in my life, I sought to replace Bob Goodman's affection anywhere I could find it: on the highway in my tight blouse and skirt, stopping truckdrivers, climbing up into the cab, bringing their hands to my breast, my open mouth to theirs, teasing them until they realized I was only a child; jumping out of my bedroom window—Aline locked the doors at night—and running into town to meet one man or another, necking, petting, never having intercourse, stopping just before penetration.

"You're lucky you weren't raped and left to die in a ditch," said Dr. G. I learned of the danger I had been in when I was well out of it.

I drank to loosen my morality, drilled into me by Aline. Nice girls do not do anything with boys until they are married. Unreasonable standards, impossible restrictions for me. I wanted a man's arms, his lips, his hands all over me, his mouth on mine or on my body, the feel of any man, the hardness of him, his response, his need of me, his love that was not love. I became whole with a man, any man. The pain stopped. And began again when he, whoever he was, was gone.

I thought I was sick, that I had a disease that did not show except through my sexuality. The pattern began with an extreme, excessive need to be with a man and ended in an abortive sexual encounter, love interrupted—as it had been with the men I loved— followed by loss, which was inevitable, ordained not by fate but by me. My choice of men as well as my treatment of them ensured that they would go away. There was not one among them I liked. The boys who were suitable in a traditional way, or inter- esting because they were bright and attractive, did not fit into the sequence of behavior I had designed for myself.

Dr. G was right, of course. I remembered a night when I had come home crying, screaming, certain I had been raped. Aline had Ben examine my panties for sperm. He found none, but my embarrassment remained acute and searing for many years. Men and sex and loss, the triple crown of my adolescence, the three-ringed circus of my growing up.

ARNOLD WEISS
Charleston, South Carolina, 1941

I HAD TO GET MARRIED before I would have intercourse. Most middle-class women of my generation were taught not to have premarital sex, or sex with a man without being in love. I have slept with men now and then whom I did not love, but I never developed a taste for it. A man's body by itself, if I do not love the man, seems foreign and unpleasant. Love is an extraordinary lens.

My virginity, by now a technicality, was lost when I was eighteen, when I married Arnold Weiss and went to live with him in a house shaped like a Quonset hut in Charleston, South Carolina. It was 1941, and America was changing to a wartime economy. Arnold was excused from military service because of a punctured eardrum. His 4-F status required him to work for the government, so he found a job at the Charleston Navy Yard as a traffic manager.

The rows of houses earmarked for civilians were dug into a mixture of sand and dried mud. The women had to sweep their floors four or five times a day to free the linoleum of the dust that flowed in through the windows and under the doors. People who lived in the area were rednecks. The men sat on their porches in the evenings with their guns laid across their knees, ready to shoot any "nigra" who, by mistake, might stray onto their property. Our only friends were an Italian couple from Brooklyn with whom we shared our discomfort at living in ugly little houses in a strange part of the country where people's beliefs were contrary to ours.

The first delivery boy who came to our house rang the bell and dropped the package of groceries outside the door. "I wanted to see if Jews have horns!" he yelled, and ran away.

Arnold was a mama's boy, a tall, Neapolitan-looking man with weakness written all over his face. We formed a classic triangle. Mrs. Weiss, the over-protective mother. Arnold, the husband-son. Me, the daughter-in-law, the other woman. Two women in love with the same boy, the boy needing both women. A pointless threesome, going nowhere, never more at odds than on our wedding night.

The wedding at the Fort Sumter Hotel was brief. Arnold's brother took the last train back to New York, and Arnold and his mother and I headed for our new home. Mrs. Weiss had plans to visit with us for two weeks although the house had only one bed-room. Each night, she slept on a couch behind a thin partition that separated the bedroom from the living room and listened to the sounds of her son's passion, her presence as undeniable as the southern heat. She could not have rendered my vagina more impenetrable if she had actually gotten out of her bed and climbed into ours and shoved her fist up between my legs in order to keep her son's penis from entering me. The woman would not allow me to have her little boy.

Despite my efforts to open myself up to my new husband, my body remained shut during this unfamiliar family struggle. Arnold, the hero, the stiff prick, was being fought over by both of the women he loved but, by the end of the week, the satisfaction of being the central character in an unholy passion play paled next to his need for sexual relief.

A shattering sound accompanied the moment of penetration, ripping apart the little house that had been, until now, almost still with Arnold's subdued groans and my whispered protests from the connubial bed. My scream hit Mrs. Weiss like a Mack truck and sent her back home to Brooklyn on the next train, where she began to plot how to get her son away from the slut. She did. Arnold and I divorced before our second anniversary. When I was much older, I fell in love once again with a mama's boy, but, this time, the woman had been dead for six years before he and I went to bed, and he was proficient in keeping the old lady where she belonged, or he had incorporated her so skillfully into the triangle that I did not notice her presence.

FUNERAL 2

ALINE'S FUNERAL looked like an opening night.
The chapel walls were lined with people three deep.
Her friends from the old days in Westchester were
there, plus the smart rich New York contingent, plus
all the servants and hairdressers and decorators, the
endless assortment of people she had charmed over
her short, forty-six-year life. She was one of two important people in my life who was nice to everyone,
needing approval from everyone. Someone, who was
me, served as whipping boy.

I was not Aline's daughter for nothing. I took
time picking out my wardrobe, stark black, with a
long black veil bordered in black grosgrain; a sorrow-
ful young woman on the arm of her husband, who
was quite handsome in his dark suit. To the men and
women seated in the pews, I was an enigma, distanced, gossiped about, unlike anyone else's daughter, estranged from her parents, on her own,
rebellious, believed to be promiscuous. I led the
procession down the aisle in front of Ben, an argument I had won through blackmail. I would not be at
the funeral unless I was to lead it.

I pretended to faint halfway down the aisle. Arnold's and other strong, sympathetic hands held me up until I was seated. I did not feel like fainting at all. I felt that I had come into myself from behind an immense shadow and was standing tall and bright and expectant in my own sun. When Aline died in my eighteenth year, the child in me was freed. It took forty years and a revolution to set the woman free.

MORTON KAUFMAN
New York, New York, 1943–55

I REMAINED FRANCES LOEB until I became Frances Lear, a name I like and have kept as my own. My first two husbands, Arnold and Morton, had unlovely first names and not pretty last names. I have known men with nice-sounding names, but I did not marry them. Morton Kaufman or Kauffman or Kaufmann—I cannot remember how to spell my second husband's name—probably had the worst of the three names, and I liked him the least. Morton was a printing salesman who worked now and then and was, despite the fact that he was short and round and had spaces between his teeth, a womanizer.

I lived a good portion of my second marriage standing at the bar in Toots Shor's restaurant, which served the best roast beef and herring with sour cream in New York. You went to The Turf for the cheesecake, but you ate dinner and drank at Toots Shor's. The mob ate there. Hollywood stars ate there. The sports greats ate there. Phil Smit, an intermittent lover, and I had eaten there. Morton drank there every night of the week, standing at the bar, moving his womanizing eye around the room, until it landed on something he liked.

"Hello there, I'm Morton Kaufman (or Kauffman or Kaufmann). Aren't you Smit, the lithographer who's getting all the business in town?"

"Not really. Thanks for the hello." Phil turned away.

Morton kept on. "Do you mind if I sit down? Please have a drink on me. And who is the little lady?"

The little lady, asshole, is mine. "This is Frances Loeb."

I remained Frances Loeb, but I did marry Morton, and I kept up with him, drink for drink, until drinking became a serious problem, easy for anyone like me, with manic-depressive illness, hung over each morning, not even remembering the night before, blacking out. If I had sex with Morton, it was not memorable enough to break through the haze of drink. We lasted less than a year.

The last time we were together, I came home from work during lunch hour, unusual for me, to change my shoes. Morton was in our bed with some woman, and, since I was paying half the rent and we were still married, I told him and her to get out. I may have been losing the worst scum of the earth, and I probably was, but loss is loss to me. I did not know what else to do to end the pain, so I put my head in the oven and turned on the gas. It was my first suicide attempt and it was primitive and it lasted only a few minutes. Morton came back, saw what I was up to, ran out of the apartment, and returned with two policemen, who found me trying to die. It is against the law in New York to take your own life, so I was locked up in Bellevue Psychiatric Hospital. If one can get through three weeks of incarceration in that hell, one can get through anything.

BELLEVUE

WILL YOU COME TO TEA on the forty-eighth of May? Yes, yes, I answered. I am especially congenial at the end of long winter months, slopping coffee, wearing gauze. Will you speak to us of what you have learned? No, of course not, I replied, it is what I can foresee that is of value. Can you really tell the future? Yes, I assured them, underestimating neither their disbelief nor my ability to deliver.

I know, I began, that I shall go up and down and up and down and up and down and up and down, and this must be boring to you unless you are going up and down and up and down with me. Then it is not boring. Then it is one unboring fact of the future. It is not a maybe fact or a questionable or an iffy or a probable fact; it is a true fact. And, my friends, I have more to tell. In the future, I will go mad. The light around my head will fade away. The children will stop playing. Lovers will pause in their lovemaking. When I go mad, the world will observe the occasion. Someone going mad is not only a fact of the future, it is an opportunity for you to back up and be grateful for what you are not.

There were three times too many patients for the space. The beds were lined up in the corridors against walls once painted white, now deep brown-yellow with age. The floors were dark gray linoleum, almost black, dulled by years of mopping with harsh chemicals and rutted from use. Many of the women were old and talked to themselves and were frightening in their withdrawal from reality. The ward, which consisted of large rooms and two main corridors, was locked and opened by a matron when the attendants and nurses arrived in the morning and when they went home at night. The windows were barred. Nothing sent by families was allowed in. The tiny, square, padded cells for the women who were out of control took up one end of the corridor, and we could hear their screams. The lesbians had a room to themselves and slept in bunk beds crammed up against each other. Narrow paths were cleared for passage down the middle and at the sides. The women yelled filthy words at each other all night. There was a section for women who were separated from their children. The human suffering in that room was greater than in all the other rooms combined.

We ate meals at long tables, which the attendants patrolled so that we would not throw food. I could not eat the mess they put in front of me, and this refusal went down on my record. There was nothing to do all day and all night except walk the halls in bathrobes without belts (in case we decided to hang ourselves). The robes seemed filthy because of their muddy color, even though they were washed each week. We were allowed to smoke three times a day in one little room that smelled of stale butts. Showers were allowed twice a week in stuccoed, three-foot-square rooms with an attendant looking on. Once a week, she poured a foul-smelling delousing liquid over our heads and pubic hair.

A young girl in my ward stood out from the other women. She was quite lovely and seemed to be bright but terribly anxious. I asked if I could sit down beside her. If it were not for this girl, I would not have gotten through my time at Bellevue.

The patients did not talk to each other. We were afraid to talk, afraid that our feelings would come out, that we would say what we really felt. Then we would be punished, locked in solitary confinement or transferred to the state hospital where no woman is ever set free. A few were given shock therapy or drugged into addiction. Instead of psychotherapy, which did not exist there, forms were filled out with our case histories and moved from one office, or one hopeless site, to another.

Once a week we were given paper and crayons, not pencils. Pencils were sharp and could be used as weapons against ourselves or others. We drew pictures of scenes that we remembered. Many were grotesque. There were visits now and then from the doctors. They came in groups and questioned us, one by one. When my turn came, I knew that my entire future was at stake in that slit of time and space. I made myself into what I thought was expected in a person who was not insane. I stood straight and tall, my arms down at my sides, my hands unclenched, and responded to their questions in a pleasant voice, with well-thought-out answers. I told the panel of disinterested men that I hoped I would get out soon so I would not lose my job. They nodded to each other and did not send me to the state hospital. I had snowed them. Underneath my surface calm hid a terrorized, hysterical woman who was in the grip of psychosis.

Dr. G signed a statement accepting responsibility for me, and I was discharged, but all the other women, even the young girl, were sent to the state hospital and remained there until they went insane or died.

THE COPA

BY THE TIME I was released from Bellevue, I had, indeed, lost my job. I needed money right away, so I applied for work at the Copacabana nightclub as a camera girl. My hours were six p.m. to two a.m., so I had all day for interviews for a better job that I would be fired from in a year or two for insubordination.

"Good evening, this is Barry Gray. I'm at the Copa. Where are you?"

Gray was in the lounge doing his radio show. If you had your hearing, if you were out of your crib, if you were affluent enough to afford a radio, you recognized Barry Gray's voice and you knew about the Copa. The Copa had the best show of any nightclub in New York. The headliners were the great singers and comedians from all over the world. Tall, gorgeous women danced in the chorus line. Some were high-ticket call girls, most went home to their husbands after the last show. The tourists who packed the room each night were overcharged for each drink, each cup of coffee. They paid to get in, to get a table, and they slipped the captain five dollars on their way out.

The mob owned the place, the mob ran it, the mob got the best tables, the best service, the best girls, and all the profit. The New Yorkers who went there were big tippers, the nouveau riche, the not-so-classy crowd, cloak-and-suiters who made fortunes during the war, Texas oilmen with models on their arm, spoiled young Long Island couples out on the town, show business folk who came for the acts, honeymooners, celebrants of all kinds of occasions. The Copa was the best-run clip joint in New York.

Before going to work at the Copa, we had to be fingerprinted and licensed at the police station and then get past the boss. I have worked for a lot of people and have known a lot of men, but there was no one like Jack Entratter. He was the best person at his job I ever knew. I learned about leadership and precision and responsibility and decision-making and how fast a man's reflexes can be from Jack Entratter, who was huge, ugly, and a glass-slick operator. He appeared not to like anybody who worked with him, or to trust anyone, especially an employee. He yelled if we were an inch beyond the red line, backstage, where we stood during the show. He could have run the Army, the Navy, and the Marines, gagged, hog-tied, and stuffed in the trunk of a car.

The men and women who checked hats and took pictures of the guests were expected to cheat. They were paid less than minimum wage, but with tips and stealing they got by. The hatcheck scam was easy: a quarter (in those days) for the house, another quarter for the house, a quarter for the checker. Checking hats was the most lucrative job for a woman, next to being in the chorus. The waiters were men. The camera girl was the lowest-ranking employee and the lowest paid with the least opportunity to steal. A flash photo of me, framed in heavy-coated stock with the logo of the Copa, reveals that I was in trouble with myself, in trouble with the world.

Entratter's minions came to the darkroom on surprise visits to count the supplies, so the man who developed the pictures used his own paper and supplies—previously sneaked into the club—once or twice an evening, and reported one or two fewer pictures than were actually taken. We split the difference, and I gave him half my tips.

The worst part of my job was hearing the same thing from almost every customer I approached.

"May I take your picture, sir?"

"Sorry, honey, I'll break your camera."

And the other one.

"Would you like to have your picture taken, sir?"

"Ask my wife." She would say no and she was not his wife.

Before the club opened every night, Entratter checked the length of our skirts, the seams in our stockings, our makeup, our hair, the neatness of our uniforms. If anything was even an eighth of an inch out of place, he would roar like a jet taking off and swing his fat arms in the air, reducing us to dust. I was more afraid of Jack Entratter than of any policeman, any disease, any act of God. I was partially paralyzed by him after he yelled at me for being five minutes late on the night Frank Costello came in for dinner and the show.

Costello, a mob leader, was in the middle of a highly publicized 1951 Senate investigation. He did not allow his face on television but could not prevent the cameras from focusing on his hands while he was testifying. There were pictures of his hands on every front page. It was very dramatic. Frank Costello looked like a mobster, talked like a mobster, but that night, when he was sitting at a table, doing nothing, waiting for the opening act, he looked like just another Joe.

"Would you like to have your picture taken, sir?"

Before the "sir" was out of my mouth, Entratter's hands had grabbed me under my armpits, lifted me two feet in the air, and carried me, in exactly the same position and height from the floor, out into the street, set me down, and kissed me goodbye.

"Try another line of work, kid."

Walking home alone at two a.m. from the Copa on Sixty-first Street to my apartment in a brownstone on Seventy-second Street was safer than approaching Frank Costello. If I had recognized him and snapped a picture, which I automatically did with celebrities, I would have been dead within twenty-four hours.

I WANTED TO BE a journalist, but I did not have the education or the experience, and it was a rare woman who was paid to be a reporter in the 1940s. Salesgirl was a more available entry-level job. I was hired by B. Altman for $22.50 a week and assigned to the better blouse department. A sign marked CLEAR-ANCE indicated a rack of reduced merchandise in the middle of the floor. When asked by a customer to show her a few styles in her size, I turned to the rack and said, "We have some Clarence blouses." The memory of the first time I opened my mouth at work, which should have taught me the value of keeping it shut, embarrasses me still. My salary precluded my staying at a hotel, so I moved in with two young women I had met in school: one earned $18.00 as a receptionist, the other took home $20.00 every Saturday from Lanz of Salzburg. The three of us lived in one room and bathed, cooked, and did our laundry in the bathroom. We had one good dress among us and it was worn only on dates. If the date was a lover, or likely to become one, the two who were dateless went to the park or some other place that was free of charge. The roommate who made $18.00 went home every weekend and brought back food that we ate all week. I was soon fired from Altman's, which gave me the opportunity to find a job in an industry other than retailing and cosmetics where most women worked. *The American Banker,* a small financial newspaper, hired me for less than I had made at Altman's, but the job was in a prestigious company on Wall Street. My duties included taking classified ads, which I later listed on my résumé as advertising sales experience. After *The American Banker* hit hard times and eliminated my job, I moved uptown to Ciro Parfums, where I was the receptionist and switchboard operator. My work was very boring. To amuse myself, I listened in to the boss's phone conversations, was discovered, and fired. Roy Durstine had been a partner at BBD&O, an advertising agency, but something happened that split up the partnership, and he went into business for himself. His offices were beautiful, and there was a huge, smartly furnished waiting room where I sat in my new job as receptionist. After a few months, I was promoted to typist, then to assistant to the assistant production manager, who soon got a better position in another advertising agency. I was promoted to his job. The production manager was a very dear man who smoked a pipe all day. I learned a great deal from him about reproducing ads. He taught me how to specify type and took me to a loft to see how silk screening was done. He explained halftones and the basics of color and printing and paper, and he never laid a hand on me. Mr. Durstine called me into his office once when a group of men were standing around looking at a layout for an advertisement for Seagram's. Mr. Durstine, who had never spoken to me before this moment, asked me if the woman in the ad was properly dressed. I was terrified. The woman was less than an inch high and she had on a horrible dress. I lied and said the dress was beautiful. I was fired anyway a few months later. In the advertising business, long multi-martini lunches were common, and I drank through them once too often. I took my experience at the agency and hyped it a little and got a job as advertising manager at A. S. Barnes, a sports book publisher, where I met many champions. Among them was the great athlete Babe Didrikson. I was fired from that job because I hated to write advertising copy and it showed. Finally, I had to admit that it was hard for a woman to get anywhere in a man's world, so I went back to retailing and was hired for the training squad at Bloomingdale's by the head of personnel, who later became a Secretary of Labor. Although I was much older than the young men and women just out of college who were normally hired for the squad and, although I had only a high school education, my work experience made up for these shortcomings. When I was fired from Bloomingdale's, I went to Saks Fifth Avenue, where I was told that I would not fit into the culture. Lord & Taylor thought better of me, but the only job they had in the whole store was for a stock girl in the bathing suit department. I spent my days in the stockroom matching bras to bottoms and fixing zippers and hanging up merchandise. Harold Krensky, then vice president and merchandise manager of Bloomingdale's, visited Dorothy Shaver, the president of Lord & Taylor, and he asked her about a former employee of his. Personnel located me in the bathing suit stockroom. I have rarely been as proud as I was that day when two of the great merchants in New York came looking for me, as Mr. Krensky put it, "to see how you're doing." They said hello, stayed less than a minute, and left, but I knew it was an omen. When I resigned from Lord & Taylor to get married, I was the buyer for better active sportswear, a high-fashion department. Ms. Shaver said I was getting out of the business just in time. "Frances, when I retire, the merchandise men will run the store, and the great days of fashion will be over." I bought a word processor in the 1970s and called myself—to myself—the Grandma Moses of the short piece. A "My Turn" essay in *Newsweek* was my first published writing. There were some other pieces in magazines and newspapers. One about corporate resistance to affirmative action was rewritten by, and printed in, the *Harvard Business Review*. There were other unimportant jobs, such as selling turquoise-and-silver jewelry in Reno when I was getting my divorce from Arnold, temporary positions as receptionist or typist or secretary between good jobs, several starts where the boss's libido was an unsolvable problem. In my first entrepreneurial venture—Lear, Purvis, Walker & Co., an executive-search firm specializing in women and minorities—I teamed up with a black woman and a black man, affirmative action incarnate, and failed. I have worked without pay in presidential elections and in off years as well, in organizations dedicated to the cause of women, in behalf of victims of child abuse, incest, and mental illness. I drew the line at the PTA.

DR. G WAS EXPLICIT, firm, unprofessional, and in violation of the IRS when demanding payment for his psychiatric services.

"You will pay me in cash on the first of every month. I don't care if you have to whore for the money." A friend had recommended Dr. G. My illness was running my life. Uncontrolled periods of mania were followed by weeks of overwhelming despair. I was desperate for help at any price.

My assistant buyer's salary, substantially under ten thousand dollars, bore no resemblance to the total of my bills for Galanos sample dresses direct from the showroom, rent for a one-room ground-floor apartment on East Thirty-eighth Street with a fireplace and twelve-foot ceilings, upscale vacations complete with new clothes, and a garage for my car. I lived at a level of extravagance that I could not afford. So whore I did, high-class whoring, but whoring it was. Dr. G, too, was a whore. He had me sexually. I paid him in cash.

To accommodate my expensive taste and to abate my terror of poverty, it was necessary, on occasion, not without serious reflection, never without some loss of self-respect, to sell out. I never compromised my political beliefs or my dreams for the world, but everything else has been on the block. That is the way it was when I met Phil Smit.

Phil Smit was the best lithography salesman in the business. The combination of his tough business acumen and the sweetness of his disposition made him attractive to me. He was certainly unattractive physically, but there was something in him that was comfortable, familiar. The trade-off was my affection and body in return for economic security. I did not know when the relationship would end, but I knew it was I who would end it, not Phil. Someday I would have a man to love.

Like many men beyond draft age, Phil made a great deal of money during the war. New-rich, pretentious, crass, Phil was not my kind of person. Nor was he easily generous. When I fell in love with a fur-trimmed red wool suit in a Fifth Avenue window while we were out walking, he made certain that I liked it.

"Do you really want the suit?"

"It's absolutely gorgeous. I'd adore it." I was thrilled that he might buy it for me.

Phil hailed a cab. We went to his apartment, had sex, went back to the store, and he bought me the suit.

We lived in a non-negotiable state of quid pro quo, tit for tat, you get yours and I get mine. I moved into his apartment for a few months, and lived with him, on and off, for ten years. Monogamy is a stellar proposition and I have lived it all my life, but I think now that I was wrong. Rarely is anyone permanently all there is for another, certainly not Phil Smit for me, not even for ten minutes.

Phil's falling in love with me was a surprise to both of us, a painful experience for him, a burden for me. I tried to love him; I had never been so secure. His love for me dug deep into my fears and lessened them. We almost married three times. I still have the rings he gave me, each more elaborate than the one before, each more expensive.

The morality that has clung to me was not always operative and was not evident in my relationship with Phil, but he was the best of my deal-making with men. The cost to me was time. I was waiting for a man with whom I wished to have children, a man who would be a permanent father. I had proof that a woman whose father does not stick around lives with a sword at her side and must, for all of her future, for each of her days, fight demons. A girl child without a father has a leg up on, is perhaps better off than, a boy child without a mother, but that is not saying much for either. The prognosis for such children varies, depending upon the child's grit and tissue and degree of magic.

I would not have children with Phil, not only because I did not love him but because I knew that I would leave him when the war he did not fight was over—before the eighteen years that stretched between us made him old, before my body softened and I would be unable to find the best of men to love permanently—when the man I would marry was home from overseas.

Permanence and I are not bedfellows. Making book against my loving Norman Lear permanently, beyond the years of my children's childhoods, and on into the years when I would grow old, was easy. I would have bet against it myself.

BISEXUAL MEN AND WOMEN, at least those I have
known, are full of sex. I have been involved three
times with women sexually, but I do not believe that
makes me lesbian or especially masculine as a woman
or anything but admiring of and drawn to women,
their bodies, and the warmth and ease with which
they communicate.

Provincetown, Massachusetts, and Fire Island
and Greenwich Village in New York were, and pos-
sibly still are, the centers of homosexuality in the
Northeast, and by chance, I lived at one time or another in all three places. But no sexual experience do
I remember more affectionately than the hours I
spent with a woman in Paris. She made known her
interest in me when her hands stroked my thigh in a
charming low-key nightclub not far from where I was
staying at the Hotel Meurice in the first *arrondisse-
ment* on a buying trip for Lord & Taylor. I was
thirty-one. My room, overlooking the Tuileries with
its long rows of red and yellow tulips, was tiny, with
barely enough space for a wardrobe and a bed that
was bigger than a twin but smaller than a double,
puffed half as high with linen as it was wide. As once

before, at seventeen, when I was seduced by a lesbian in Provincetown, I was unable to give the other woman dominance or control. The physicality of women begs for undefined roles between them. My French friend allowed me to act in any way I wished. I did not feel like a man nor did she seem to mind that I was not one. Both of us were unaware of difference or sameness, both acted on the same impulses without designations of active or passive, or him or her, or anything more than the exchange of affection and sexual passion between two free creatures. We had oral sex, which gave me pleasure. The gratification in oral sex for men when performed by women, or for women when performed by men, is obvious. Now I could understand the sensual enjoyment men receive, more subtle, lovely, intimate. A woman making love to another woman is without clutter. It is also egalitarian.

Virginia E was a professor of literature and drama, fiftyish, delicate, with spun golden hair mixed with white. I studied with her at college the summer I worked part-time as secretary to the dean. That fall I went to room with her in her walk-up apartment on Thirty-fourth Street. Virginia taught me to read books, what books to read, why I should read them, and that reading would ultimately give me freedom. I had not learned the value of literature in elementary school or in the second-rate boarding schools I attended through the twelfth grade. I was a dropout (a term unknown in those days) in my first year of college, when I was sixteen. Troubled, a loner, I could not concentrate on my studies. People like me who are literate but without formal education are often described as self-educated, but that is not true. We have lived a long time, and one gathers information over time, like the gathering of dust.

Virginia and her homosexual friends, Jerry and Kermit, and I, straight, but as much an outsider as they, spent time together as a family. We celebrated birthdays and holidays, particularly Christmas, when Virginia's shabby living room was transformed into a wonderland of pine cones and popcorn garlands and was filled with the rich aroma of mulled wine. The Christmas tree drooped the night it was decorated, its branches heavy with ornaments. Before the two men arrived in the morning, we layered the floor beneath with presents. Jerry got a new pipe from Virginia each year, and the two men would buy me a tasteful, extravagant piece of clothing. I would amuse the three of them at dinner with my stories about men, about the merchandise manager at Lord & Taylor who took me home after the Christmas party, when I learned how little some men require in bed.

Virginia, Kermit, and Jerry were the best surrogate parents I ever had, and they gave me a source of inspiration from which I still take reinforcement. They were the first adults to make me believe that I was more than my appearance, that I had intelligence.

The people of my own age whom I chose as friends were like my image of myself. My girlfriend Jette was as shallow as the water where I once went bone fishing in the Florida Keys.

The love that Virginia felt for me was far beyond my understanding. It was oftentimes silly, sometimes inappropriate. Her apartment was divided into a living room, a Pullman kitchen, a bath, and a small bedroom. I slept on the couch.

"You need more rest," said Virginia, and gave up her bed to me.

She went to the movies whenever I was entertaining a man. She spent all her free time educating me. She cooked—my favorite was her potato-leek soup—and she cleaned. She refused to go away on vacation because she did not want me to be alone in the apartment. She sopped up my ill temper and would not give me the discipline I needed. Once every few months, a man from Philadelphia came to see her. That night, it was my turn to go to the movies.

The world, myself included, saw in Virginia a spinster woman who had waited all her life for a child and had found one, grown up, in her student. But I learned, at the end of my five-year stay, that Virginia was after something else. I thanked her, a simple thank you, no more than Thank you, Virginia, for the haven you have given me, and I touched her as a lover for lack of another way to express my deep feelings for her. She was wet instantly. How long had she waited for such a moment? I do not know, but I suspect it was all of her adult life, just as she had waited for a child. I never touched her again, and I soon moved away, but I hoped she would keep the memory of me as both child and lover for the rest of her life.

months of
An hour
s brains
ght.
n for
in a
es,
ke
r

JNG, I thought I was a nympho-
lks that, you know, if one doesn't have
y lovers were competent enough, but I
n up; me, a solid, stolid mass of female, not
certainly, wet and warm of vagina, cold of
Inside my brain played a wax recording of No,
't, no, don't, no, don't, no, don't—Aline's voice—
o, don't, no, don't. I obeyed her, and remembered
my stepfather's fingers, and did not for most of my
life.

Sidney Fast was a pock-faced great tree of a man who could not make a living outside the military. He wrote poetry to me when he was at sea, but his real talent was his prowess in bed. Neither the conflicts of his childhood, nor being out of place in the world beyond the United States Navy, nor the conditional nature of my love for him, interfered with his sexual appetite or performance. He knew that I was angry at men, that I faked orgasm.

After being stationed aboard the aircraft carrier *Kearsarge* for three years during World War II, Sidney became deeply depressed and was sent to the

naval hospital at Bethesda. He received six
shock therapy before he was discharged.
after he left the hospital grounds, he blew h
out in a pawnshop with a pistol he had just bo

I worked at reaching orgasm with other m
many years after Sidney died, but frigidity
woman can be exorcised only by extreme measu
since the best revenge for a woman's anger is to ma
a man feel inadequate in bed. Getting rid of ange
toward men requires a woman to die. When she dies,
the anger dies with her. The trick, of course, is to
come back from death after the job is done, after all
the pertinent memories and faces have become
blanks. I am here to assure you that resurrection is a
real possibility, because I have died and come back.
Sometime during the period of my death, I took my
rage and threw it out the window. This kind of death
is not the ending of life but is the changing of oneself, as in the often heard phrase "I am not the same
person."

MARCEL AUBRY

A WOMAN IS GIVEN a chance to right the past if she loves a man who is old enough to be her father. Her relationship with her dad is reborn and made whole, made perfect, as she would have wanted it in childhood, but she pays a price for this manipulation, especially if she is responsive to aesthetics.

I loved an investment banker who was thirty years my senior. Marcel Aubry was more beautiful than Maurice Chevalier though not as beautiful as Yves Montand, but he was as French as both of them with his waxed, sculptured mustache, conservative dark suits from Savile Row, Patek Philippe watch, handmade shirts, most of them silk, all of them white. He carried a cane and always wore a hat. He was graceful and lean, dignity itself. I adored him. One day he took me to lunch at an exquisite French restaurant, La Crémaillère. Charles Boyer, the most beautiful Frenchman of them all, was already seated at our table. The men talked in French. I sat, dumb-struck, in heaven.

Marcel made a fortune buying and then selling Nedick's, the chain of hot-dog stores. On the day the sale was completed, he took me to a Ford showroom and bought me a red convertible, which I drove until many years later when my husband and I traded it in for a secondhand blue Chevrolet. Marcel was seldom generous with material things; he never gave me money, but he gifted me with knowledge and know-how and sophistication and advice and pure appreciation of, and pleasure in, his love for me. Marcel Aubry was my Professor Higgins. He taught me how to handle money, how to behave at work, and he tried, unsuccessfully, to make me control my temper. He believed that I had the potential for a successful career, that I had talent. He told me how to behave with the men I was seeing. We lunched several times a week and took long walks in the early evenings before he went home. We talked about his son, whom he loved more than anyone, and his wife, his business, his worries, his pleasures. We talked to each other about everything that was in our hearts and in our heads, and, on occasion, we talked about our fantasies. We thrilled each other and we flirted constantly. We did not make love, having tried it once. As we lay down together on the bed in my one-room apartment, we knew we had made a mistake and ended the episode at once, before we touched. Some men—Marcel was one—cannot have sex with children. I was too young, too dull, too inexperienced for him. That same year he was having an affair with his wife's best friend. His wife was having an affair with her too. I imagined the three of them together. They were way out of my league.

Before that day in my apartment, I had looked at Marcel a thousand times, imagining his body, knowing how different it surely was from Morton's body or Arnold's body or any body I had known. The attraction that young women feel for well-established older men is substantial. Wisdom and wealth are heady stuff for a woman, as is the proximity of youth for a man, but there is a serious obstacle. A woman cannot look sexually at a man who is old enough to be her father without being startled, without feeling that this body is somehow strange, not right to touch —even if she has experienced incest as a child. It is not a matter of morality. It is simply an aesthetic.

I would have married Marcel and lived the remaining years of his life with him, for no man before or since has made me feel so admired. I see my feelings for Marcel mirrored in the faces of young women married to older men, and I know their secret. They have crafted a perfect circle of their lives. They have taken the good from the past and added it to the good in the present and, if they need more than that, they sleep with beautiful young men in the afternoon.

HAROLD KRENSKY

THERE ARE TWO Harold Krenskys. The one
who was the vice president and merchandise manager
of Bloomingdale's before his son died and the one I
hugged in a coffee shop in Santa Monica, California,
years after he had retired from retailing. You could
tell the second one had once been handsome, but his
face was puffy now and his body was thick in the
middle where it once had been hard and slim. His
bearing was that of a man who had succumbed to
tragedy. I could almost feel his broken heart.

I first saw Harold Krensky on the escalator in the
main store in New York when I was the assistant
buyer for junior dresses and sportswear. The rate of
his descent from the floor above gave him time to
look over the floor below—the displays, the neatness
of the piles and racks of merchandise, the appearance
of the salesgirls. When Krensky did his three-times-
a-day inspections, backs straightened and smiles appeared. You could feel the crack of energy across the
floor as the staff responded to the elegance of his
carriage, the brightness of his face. A woman had to
be stone cold dead not to respond sexually to Harold
Krensky. Ida Sciolino, my boss, emerged flushed and

alive, a woman in love, after their meetings in his office. I think Krensky was faithful to his beautiful wife—he appeared to be, and there was never any gossip otherwise—although many women, myself included, did not stop believing they would, one day, have sex with him.

On Thursdays, when Bloomingdale's stayed open late, I chose a dress from stock and modeled it in front of the escalators to draw attention to the department. The store was always crowded at night, but I did not miss seeing Z. Rita Watts—the psychiatrist who had repeated my confession to Aline and Ben—as she passed in front of me. I approached her.

"My name is Frances Loeb. Do you remember me?"

"I think so, young lady. What do you want?"

I accused her of having betrayed me and her profession.

"Get out of my way. I always thought you were crazy."

The embarrassment I felt at my impulsive accusation, delivered at the head of the escalator in the rush of Thursday-night shopping, reinforced my rage toward psychiatry.

I learned retailing in the days before IBM tickets with their bewildering little holes hung on every garment, before daily sales printouts were used for reordering instead of the experience and expert judgment of the women who bought for the fashion departments, before these buyers were turned into mere order takers, before the male merchandise managers selected fashion according to the bottom line, before the surge of MBAs into department store retailing signaled the end of the industry.

Long before mentoring became a buzzword in the women's movement, I was mentored by Harold Krensky as men are mentored by other men, not just by the passing of knowledge from one mind to another but—or was it my imagination?—with the tacit belief that I would one day reach a high position in the company. I had worked in advertising, publishing, and assorted other businesses, but retailing was Mecca to a woman like me with little education and an eye for fashion. Women were powerful in retailing. Called "big pencils," we wrote orders for many thousands of dollars and were feted and flattered and often seduced for the business we gave away.

A man and two women taught me retailing. Krensky taught me strategy and management by the example he set. Ida Sciolino inspired me and pushed me and told me everything she knew about fashion and merchandising, and believed in me and still does, I think, to this day. Ida was a tiny woman with an immense brain who helped to originate junior-size clothes for women. She married a man in the jewelry business and had a son and lived happily ever after.

The other woman was Marjorie Griswold, who trained me when I worked as a buyer at Lord & Taylor. After decades at the store, Marjorie retired to a one-room apartment and lived on the little money she had been able to save for food and housing for herself and her cat. Marjorie Griswold's memory remained with me in the sharpest detail and in its full meaning. I would not grow old in poverty. I would marry and be financially secure. I would not risk a fate like Marjorie's with the dream of becoming Krensky's heir.

Bloomingdale's required a two-year stint at a branch store as one of the steps to buyer. I was assigned to a department as manager in the Fresh Meadows store. I hated being there. The drive back and forth each day from New York City meant traffic jams on the parkways and the added cost of commuting, which the store did not absorb. The departments were small. Business was slow, dreadfully slow, in comparison to the action in the main store in the city. I was bored. Merchandise was shipped to me whether I wanted it or not, so I had no power over the department's performance. I longed to return to New York.

Martha Fuchs was the ready-to-wear manager. I remember her as an ordinary-looking woman of medium height and weight, close to fifty years of age, and tough as a steel girder. She seemed to dislike me because I was thin and young, and she resented the fact that Krensky, who was her boss too, stayed a long time in my department, talking, whenever he visited the store.

My guess is that I was in the middle of a severe change of mood, going down to a depression, on the day I yelled at Martha Fuchs in front of customers and other employees. Something had to have been off track in my head for me to act in such an outrageous manner, then to jump in my car, speed to New York, and burst into Krensky's office.

"It's her or me!"

Krensky, who had been telephoned about the incident, looked at me with disappointment and disbelief that I could throw away such a good career opportunity, that I could have acted in so irresponsible and uncontrolled a manner, that his faith in me meant so little that I would not put up with an ordinary asshole for just two years, that this was the end of his hopes for me. From the look on his face, I saw the end of my dreams for myself. He sat behind his desk, cupping his chin in his hand in his customary manner, and looked deep into my eyes with an affection that felt to me like love.

"It's you, Frances."

The next week I went to work for Lord & Taylor, but there was no Harold Krensky on the escalator, only an ordinary merchandise manager who was not beautiful and not much interested in my career. He was after my body, which is another kind of job security.

I lost more than a career when, five years later, I left Lord & Taylor to marry Norman Lear. The work

I did, the proof of my ability, the establishment of my credibility, all were and still are the material on which I assess myself. I gave up my self-esteem twice in my life—once when I left retailing and put aside my role as a worker and, again, after I had my daughters, when I stayed too long out of the work force.

JERRY LEWIS
Las Vegas, Nevada, 1955

THE VOICE IN MY HEAD that is lodged in the right rear quadrant of my brain, barely below the skull, was not confused. Nor is it ever confused. Brief cogent phrases issue from it, enunciated as Richard Burton might have spoken them or, if sung, as Julie Andrews would have crafted them into pearl shapes and crystal sounds. The voice in my head is experience and reason. It is always right and I do not listen to it. I listen to my gut.

There is nothing glamorous in the duplex apartment that is reserved for the headline performer who is booked into the Desert Inn in Las Vegas. The square footage is impressive and there is a piano in the living room, but the rooms smell of the stars who live in them, and there is still a faint odor of Jerry Lewis from his last trip. The inside of a star's narcissism smells like no other smell. It is nasty and strong.

My date was in Nevada for the required six-week residence to obtain a divorce. On my visit, we saw all the great performers and went to Jerry's duplex to congratulate him after his show. I heard a man on the receiving line tell Jerry how great his performance was, that Jerry was never funnier in his whole life, that Dean had been a noose around his neck, how much the audience loved him, that he was the best stand-up comic in the business. The ease with which he obviously lied and the way Jerry Lewis drank in the lie made me understand the place of lying in show business. Lying is not a moral issue in the entertainment world. It is a prop to hold up entertainers who cannot ever get off the stage, or producers and directors who want to get on it, who need applause in the bathtub. Narcissists are by definition empty inside.

When it was my turn to congratulate the star, I stood and looked at that extraordinarily well-paid, nationally loved face and could say nothing that had not been said or that was not a lie. No sound came from me because almost anyone in his or her right mind can tell when I am lying, and even if someone is expecting me to lie, it comes out so twisted and aborted that it ultimately takes shape as an insult. Frozen with embarrassment, I half smiled, said nothing, and moved on. It is true that performances of the kind put on by the man who lied to Jerry Lewis are required in show business. Fawning becomes reflexive, and most people, including myself, become taken with the idea of being fawned over.

The nature of fame was unknown to me when I met Jerry Lewis. One cannot expect fame itself to warn us of its nature, but the ill effect of its presence on everyone in the room was as glaring as the Las

Vegas summer noonday sun. The voice in my head, not the one in my gut, sprang to attention, aware that performing is not my forte, certain that I could not develop the skill. It said no in the perfect diction of Richard Burton. Don't, trilled Julie Andrews, lips in a perfect o. "Don't go into show business," ordered the voice calmly, speaking from its ancient knowledge. "You do not belong there. Blow the limousine, Frances. Take a trolley. Walk."

FRANCES LEAR

MARRIAGE
Los Angeles, California, 1956–85

I

My life is like an epic poem
With lines that rhyme with he and she.
He is what I might have been
And she is only me.

II

ONE OF THE GENERIC NAMES for show business is Hollywood, and it extends from the San Fernando Valley to Santa Monica to downtown Los Angeles, for legal and financial matters, and as far east as Pasadena. The tropical air, fresh and floral-scented in the days before pollution, begs to be gulped and held in. Masses of vivid bougainvillea color the sides and roofs of the houses in the neighborhoods where my family and our friends lived. Lush green lawns blanket the great expanses between the front doors and the broad clean streets. In time, one becomes accustomed to the malodor of fear that drives the men in the industry.

It leaks through the freshly painted homes decorated with large white sofas and specially woven rugs. The same human musk emanates from the damp tuxedo collars of the executives and second-rate talent who attend the industry affairs.

I I I

The truth about people is obfuscated in Hollywood because the town is populated with fabrications. The folks who live there spend a great deal of time getting their visible selves straight. Talented men and women are employed in the business of weaving tales for movies or television, trained in the invention of characters. Most of the made-up personalities are astonishingly well fashioned. There are killers who look like sweet, slightly ethnic or strongly WASP boys. There are family men who get blow jobs during lunch from actresses who are looking for work. In all the years I lived in Hollywood, I knew of only two monogamous marriages. The ups and downs of the Matterhorn are flat by comparison to the sine wave of success and failure in Hollywood.

I V

I moved from New York to California when I married at thirty-three, and made good use of the weather and the ease with which one could raise a family. I lived in a New England clapboard house amid lush jacaranda trees that bloomed into lavender-blue clouds. My daughters had skin like flan, and my husband was programmed by destiny to be a star. When my girls were old enough to board the yellow bus and go off to school, I planted flats of flowers that grew into large blossoms. I cut them and placed them in vases around the house, as Aline had done. I planted new flats every year in the spring. While my girls were at school, I sewed dresses for them and I designed and sewed shirtdresses for myself. The children outgrew their dresses and I became tired of mine. Then I designed and sewed new dresses for us and gave the old ones away. I became a gourmet cook and spent afternoons, and mornings as well, making complex meals that were eaten in less than an hour. The following night's gourmet meals were eaten in the same way. I fixed the broken toilets, which would break again. I did the tasks that people at home do, as often and as competently. All housewives live circles. Many find them pleasing and safe. Mine eventually entrapped and suffocated me.

V

I married three times in front of a judge and not one photo or one marriage remains.

V I

I hungered after Burt Lancaster for most of my life.

EARLY RETIREMENT

THE MAY COMPANY paid their buyers the highest salaries of any department store chain in the country, in exchange for a six-day work week and buying trips to New York and Europe four times a year to see the collections and to order merchandise. Thursday-night store openings were managed by assistant buyers, but an appearance by the buyer during peak selling hours impressed management.

The Los Angeles store was mammoth. Merchandise, chosen for volume selling and not for its style, was jammed into cases and loaded on racks in accordance with store policy. This retail thinking, based on the lemming principle, escalated into failure in the late 1980s. Management had underestimated the independence of the female consumer, who had become a woman with a mind and money of her own.

If I were to continue to work in California, the logical progression in my career after Bloomingdale's and Lord & Taylor would be to buy for the May Company, but, certainly, I thought, the next steps in my life were motherhood, homemaker, wife. Yet the continuing need to test my mettle in the job market, to put a price on myself in California, to increase my antipoverty insurance with a new job offer, prompted me to call for an interview at the giant store on Wilshire Boulevard. My years of experience in New York were attractive to a California-based operation. After talking to the personnel manager and the merchandising head of the fashion floor, I was asked to take over the sportswear department at a salary that was higher than I had ever expected to earn in this life.

On the scenic route home along Mulholland Drive, I thought about the hours, the travel schedule, and, after a few miles of pondering, I was afraid for my marriage, for myself, afraid that buying for the May Company would keep work as the focus of my life. I had a new focus now: a home, a husband. His career was my security. I would have children. I would live as women were supposed to live, sheltered and adored. In the swiftest and deepest and most lasting misstep of my life, I turned down the job. One person, a man, told me I was making a mistake. But I was too caught up in my new role to listen to Norman Lear.

HOLLYWOOD

IT IS A NATIONAL MONUMENT. Its meat-and-potatoes has, no doubt, already been described by other women, unknown to me, who have gone to the same parties and been divorced the same number of times. There is nothing new under the Pacific Coast sun except—to outsiders—the speed at which things repeat themselves. On the simplest level, Saturday's party will be catered by, flowered by, attended by, the same people as next Tuesday's. Only the name of the host will change—as restaurants do, or plastic surgeons, or studio heads. There is always a body or a business, cloned from the previous one, ready to step in. Names change in Hollywood; the rest stays the same.

The town seems nailed down because, within each category, everything is alike. One tract house is no different from another except for the name on the deed. Houses are identified by their owners, and the owner's name defines the taste, so architecture as an art form is missing. A house is a house. In upscale residential areas, the level of taste varies slightly, and the buildings seem self-conscious.

There is something organically, or meteorologically, wrong with the weather. Los Angeles days are sunny and bright and up, but after years of it, you feel, for no reason you can identify, that the clock inside you is in need of a new battery. I, too, had a run-down clock and, in addition, there was a very heavy, old-fashioned, nonelectric iron on top of my head. I know some energetic people in Los Angeles who never slow down, but they are impelled by fear, which is its own power plant.

Hollywood's the name, glamour's the game. True glamour does exist—Cher personifies one kind, Audrey Hepburn the opposite. The illusion of glamour, the icing for a cake that does not rise, the Band-Aid for lack of class, is manufactured by professionals with well-paying jobs. But the heat in the making of pretend, the touch of circus in every major event, the hysteria that turns nothing into something spellbinding, is provided by rank amateurs, innocents, and people like me. There is no glamour unless there is a crowd around it. The photographs that appear in print, the television bites, are of the stars and the Big Industry Names, but the adoration, the excitement, the movement, the magic, the pitch of an event—the glamour—is supplied by the faithful who live in Aberdeen, Texas, or Bangor, Maine, and in Brentwood, Bel Air, and Beverly Hills, the home of the stars and the Big Industry Names and their families. Wives go to the award shows and are kissed and hugged by the winners for all the world to see and enjoy. Those women provide an understated glamour that women all over the country identify with because it is real.

When the lights click on and the cameras, hoisted up onto thick muscular shoulders, roll outside the theater, the hotel, the studio gates, a star's home, the scene is a sequel, the ritual is played out. Some wives have names that are not the same as their husbands', some have successes of their own. New young wives stay home during the day and raise families. I found it interesting that the finest talent in the industry is at work or at home, is seldom seen at public events, and only on rare occasions gives interviews. Interesting, logical, and first-class.

The town is nailed down. The present roster of film and television stars and the new generation of important men in the industry replace mine. Names change in Hollywood; the rest stays the same.

GENETICS

KATE HAS HER FATHER'S EYES, which are blue
and seductive. Maggie's eyes are like mine, green with
grayish slivers and promises in them. All four of us
have good eyes. We are held together for all time by
distance and by disappointment and by the wondrous
feelings we have for each other. We are in love with
the laughter we experienced together, which was unlike any other. My daughters' father made humor and
I gave maternal love. My love affair with misery
began when the girls were old enough not to drown
in it.

The miracle was their existence, that I would actually give birth to a child, that I was capable of normal everything—conception, pregnancy, delivery—
that the unknown genetic tracks that preceded me and
that I had traveled would not, suddenly, in the body
of my issue, lead to unimaginable diseases and traits
and congenital poisons. A search conducted in my
twenties, back to the orphanage, to the lawyer who
served up the adoption papers, to phone books in
Hudson, New York, to look up Kraus, Krause,
Crouse, Krauss, Krouse—a name that appeared like
a ghost in an investigation by Arnold Weiss—came

up with not one medical fact, not a single clue. Eve-lyn, tell me, do you have flaws that my children will inherit?

Frances and Evelyn are united, one inside the other, and Frances assesses the strength of their combined body and the manageability of their combined mind. She is pleased. There is the flaw, of course, which figures in the total calculation, but the broken gene appears, now that it is calm, to be less a factor than the form of the features and the health of the body.

Frances did not believe in a personal God, potentially a serious complication. Her intention was to pray, or plead the case to the court of highest recourse, that her imperfection skip a generation or disappear altogether. During a time in her life when she was faintly spiritual, Frances came close to embracing the concept of a deity. A good part of her seventeenth year was spent traveling, speaking to clergy, to rabbis, to priests, to preachers, to anyone she thought might have the authority to give her faith. She yearned for a religious home, a central bank in which she could deposit her resentments and from which she could withdraw comfort. Pondering God always brought her a degree of peacefulness that was valuable and the impetus for continuing her search.

"Answers to questions concerning the existence of God," said the good men Frances queried, "come from within ourselves."

And so the journey to religious belief again led back

to her, back to square one, to blanks, to faithlessness, to the most real of realities: no recourse, no solace, no one to blame.

"There must be," she reasoned, "an order outside myself, a reason for the reasons I cannot explain, a string of words if nothing else, that would embrace my thoughts. I am a mass of no endings. I need to be grounded. I need to look up."

The answer came in time from an unlikely place, from her illness, from her conviction that life is made up of opposites, all is black and white, gray does not exist. All is good, all is bad. I am glad, I am sad. In between the two poles must be a desirable, maybe even a peaceful place, but Frances held no key to such a promised land. The best-case scenario was (1) to learn to accept the existence of a balanced state and (2) to believe in it as some believe in the power of worship. If there is balance, if the negatives and the positives live oppositely, that in itself is order, a sort of glue that keeps life from falling apart.

The nut of Frances's evolved faith was, as she was, extreme, an expectation that there would be a perfect balance in everything, in everyone. She hated the glaring omission in the liquid canals that fed chemicals and God knows what else into her brain and that, at times, outweighed her positive traits.

"But," she reasoned, "balance may not be perfect. Sanity and equilibrium may lie somewhere between the positive and the negative factors in each of us, and in the universe, although I must admit the concept is simple and *ordinary." Frances was not after originality in those days; she was interested in her legacy.*

By chance, Fate chose to take up the role of Dispenser of Goods, a job with absolute power over individual states of balance or imbalance. Fate was quite sympathetic to Frances. Her predicament seemed real. Should the young woman become pregnant? Would the fetus carry the Kraus imprint however the name was spelled? Fate, in a rebellious and sublime move, righted the genetic imbalance twice in Frances's life and made a tiny but life-altering correction on the blueprints of both her offspring.

This would have been a still happier story if fate and God had become indistinguishable in Frances's mind, considering the holiness of the gift she had received, but she could not extend her imagination into the unknown. She could not write fiction. The best she could do was sit in an empty church now and then and be peaceful and know, with a seventh or eighth sense, that the health of her children is what people call God.

THE MEN WHO LOVED ME were glued, each in his own way, to their mothers, and the principal flaw of each woman could be found tucked away within my personality, hidden in a tiny compartment, folded tight, neat, dusted, ready to unfold and lash out in a mood swing. On a descent into depression, my fears expressed themselves in anger and I would attack the vulnerability in a man that was put there by the hurtful behavior of his mother. Like most women, I was made of pieces of strength and pieces of tenderness and pieces that are not nice. Norman Lear's mother, Jeanette, was a part of me that could not be loved and was the unlovable part of him. Arnold's mother, who interfered in the course of his life and mine, was controlling; Sidney's mother was demanding. It is unsettling to know that these men found those characteristics in me. Aline was critical; so am I.

Although the mothers of the men I loved and my own mother and many other women are not good mothers, they often give life to people who are loving and good to love. My natural mother, made pregnant in some moment of adolescent abandon, was apparently not mature enough to be a good mother, but out of her womb came a generation of women who will bear yet other generations. Some among them will be fine people. Motherhood, in the long run, in its impact upon society, has most to do with the nature of the children the mothers bear.

We women should be allowed to abort unwanted pregnancies, share with men in the care and upbringing of our children, do work outside the home to gain economic independence and self-esteem. But for the life of me, no matter the damage done by her own or other mothers, I cannot understand a woman's denial of motherhood, unless there is a total absence of maternal feelings, or a physical barrier to conception or pregnancy or birth. We demand equal opportunity in the job market. Bearing children is the only franchise we have all to ourselves.

CHILDREN

MY CHILDREN gave me the chance to be what Aline was not.

THE SECOND SEDUCTION

IF I WERE STRANDED on a desert island and had to make a choice between the two kinds of fucking, I would choose mindfucking. In common usage, the term mind fucker refers to someone who manipulates other people, who fucks them over emotionally or financially. My meaning is literal. A mindfucker is a man who fucks my brains, comes on to my head so that I enjoy it. I am manipulated through my heart.

Rarely have I experienced fucking and mindfucking of the same competence with the same man. I love men for different reasons—for sex, for fun, for strength, for knowledge, for caretaking—but some who have left the strongest memories have mindfucked better than they have laid.

At the moment of its happening, sex is more important, more fulfilling than a good laugh or good talk. But for the long haul, for some of us, diddling the head can be hotter and more memorable. I have tried to equate—given the difference in real time and the extenuating circumstances in my love affairs and marriages—my memories of fucking with the collaboration of minds, and though I tend to linger over scenes of copulation, I savor the arguments that led to a better solution, the crafting of ideas together, the inching toward discovery, the wit, even the verbal horseplay.

There was a man who fucked my mind so skillfully that I may have loved him more than any other man in my life. Each time we spoke, I heard a marching band—just as I had heard it the last time we spoke and during all the times before—which would not be still even when our bodies had long since parted. His mind simply got itself into my mind, and my mind got into his, and that is the way it is for people who have been twice seduced. The first time, you fuck with your body. From then on, if you are fortunate enough to find such treasure in your life, you seduce each other's heads, you play there. You can fuck either way as often as you wish, of course, but usually people who mindfuck each other well are getting laid by someone else.

Mindfucking has nothing to do with intelligence, any more than sex has to do with physical technique, but both can generate tremendous passion. There is a host of reasons why a man and a woman choose to spend their time in the second, and often permanent, seduction. Female frigidity. Male fear of inadequacy. In a situation where both those reasons are present, mindfucking can become an art form with considerable consequence. Men and women who have mindfucked in productive collaborative marriages have, throughout history, contributed to each other in meaningful and measurable ways. They have often produced good work, though, in the past, the efforts of women were often unseen, unmarked, and even unacknowledged.

FAME
The Emmy Awards, 1972

JOHNNY CARSON was the master of ceremonies. Every seat in the Pasadena Civic Auditorium was filled. The audience glittered. Tension tightened the air. Rows of shining Emmys stood ready to be handed out. I wore a flowered beige satin Galanos gown with a silk satin stole tied in the back, and long pearl-fastened white gloves. My hair was swept up and held by a false, but perfectly matched, braid. I was in my late forties and I had never looked better, walking beside the man who was making television history, feeling pride, smiling at the bank of photographers, their lights flashing and blinding me, the perfect wife-of.

Our seats were in the eighth row. Nominees sat on the aisle, surrounded by the celebrities of television, the famous beautiful faces, the network executives and their bejeweled wives. Real diamonds and fake sparkled wall-to-wall. Heads were coiffed high, sprayed hard to the touch, dyed red or brown or bleached Monroe blond. Makeup artists and hairdressers had been rushing since early morning to Beverly Hills to Bel Air to Brentwood, making over ordinary and beautiful faces, and teasing luxuriant and inadequate hair. Favored designers, commissioned by the stars and by industry wives to make special gowns for the occasion, outdid each other's tonnages of beading and sequins. The men came in black tie or red tie or plaid tie or no tie and gathered in knots of black wool in the aisles.

The brilliant, innovative *All in the Family,* and the talented men and women who brought the series to life, had been nominated for fourteen Emmys. They won seven. When the lights went back on after the intermission and the cameras rolled, Carson, his white teeth aglow, cracked his opening line.

"Welcome to the Norman Lear Show."

The celebration party was held in a tent next to the auditorium. Excitement roared in us. We danced, we embraced, we laughed, and, in that moment, being the wife-of was transcendent. The tent was mobbed, but a path seemed to open in front of us, hands from everywhere were stretched out to be clasped, broad-smiling faces were cocked to be kissed.

The stranger who accompanied us when we entered went unnoticed by everyone but me. He was a familiar presence in Hollywood, but, until tonight, he and I had not met. He seated himself at my left. As the crowd grew larger with agents and actors and Big Industry Names congratulating, registering their presence upon the new hero, the stranger put his hand on my chair. Imperceptibly at first, inch by inch, then in spurts, he distanced me from my table, until I bumped into a woman who was seated directly behind me.

Fame is a force of its own making, slow-building or swift, infiltrating, changing molecular structures, distorting emotional truths, seeking out and attacking and destroying weak tissue. Fame, not any person, not any event, not any sum of anything done, but fame itself set my illness free and sent me into fifteen years of rapid cycling between mania and depression. This was the hole in the story that depressions pounce upon, this was the tear in the soul in which despair camps out, this was the day they gave this lady away.

The disease of lost identity had been forming slowly in me, and became acute when fame moved its goods through the front door of our home and settled in, immovable, permanent. I had been my own and every woman's fantasy. I had lived the past fifteen years like a star on the silver screen, heart-deep in the dreams of women in Iowa or Birmingham or Queens who bought movie magazines, and women who were "above" buying movie magazines but who, too, were hooked on Hollywood. My girls, my marriage, my life had brought me—traveling fast without uppers, peaceful and calm without downers—beyond the possible. I was well past fantasy. My expectations were of grandeur and bliss.

I walked down the street with the man I was the wife-of and I was recognized and greeted. I walked down the street alone and I was not recognized, nor was I acknowledged.

We had become he.

A wife-of in Hollywood does not have a name of her own, or a face that has been seen, or a voice that is ever heard, or a character that anyone reacts to, or a persona that is recalled. Exaggerated? Yes. True? Yes. The name and face and voice and character and personality of a Hollywood wife-of are so often unnoticed, not listened to, not admired, that in time she feels that she does not exist. Out of logic and necessity and love, she is worshipful of the fame that has made her its victim. A Hollywood wife-of is a paradox in the old old oldest of stories.

There was a moment in the best years of life for a woman when I stood in the bright California sun and looked down and saw that I had lost me. I had become unattached from time and place and self. My nonbeing had begun when I moved to California to marry and lived in a tiny rented apartment on Sunset Boulevard and gave myself up to the Hollywood scene, to the culture, to the need for success, to the myth of fame, to the stupid belief that fame was a friend. When fame became my enemy, and I could measure the reach of its hell-bent descent into destruction, I looked with respect at the men and women who had been offered celebrity and chosen not to accept it.

My failure to live life with an independent self interfered with the living of life by each member of my family. I became deeply depressed, a metaphor:

A small golden finely made jeweler's scale rested upon the green-felt-covered table in my stepfather's office. Flat round plates hung from either side of the scale. One held the gems; Ben piled the other plate with tiny weights shaped like chess pawns until the slender pointer at the top of the scales settled exactly in the center. The gems were of the scarcest weight and the scales were extremely sensitive, dipping swiftly in response to the slightest, most minimal, addition or subtraction on either plate.

I was on one scale, my world was on the other.

The descension and the ascension of me were as delicately balanced as the pointer on my stepfather's scale, and equally sensitive to pressure. A combination of external events and my internal nonbeing dislodged the hopelessness that lurks in manic-depressive illness. I entered years of struggle to gain a semblance of myself, to discover one stepping-stone on which I could begin to build a person I cared about, to enjoy the rewards of success, to allow the good in my life to fill me, to make inroads into the damage done to me in childhood—years of lying on couches and sitting in chairs and, almost literally, immersing myself in my past to reverse the negativism of the present.

The reasons for me to get well, to smile, to love, to live, were real and fine and all around me. The good life could not bore its way through my illness. Antidepressant medications did not work for me, and there was no escape from the environment that continued to assault my sense of myself. Progress was undone before it was set. In time, I had no alternative. I checked into a motel on Ventura Boulevard with a bottle of vodka and two full prescriptions of Seconal, swallowed both, and remained unconscious for two days before I was found.

The hospital attendant was middle-aged, gay, odd-looking, and sad. "Why did you do it?" he asked. "You have so much to live for."

He was right, I had much to live for. But none of it mattered. No one could have stopped me from trying to take my life. The pain in the depression preceding my suicide attempt was greater, by far, than my joy had been in giving birth, twice, to life.

THE MOVEMENT

IN 1963, one of the most influential women in the world wrote about the truth of my life, which I had kept fetal, unseen, even by me. Betty Friedan stripped bare my image of myself as Mrs. American Wife and Mother, exposing a cleaner of toilets, a submerser of self, wasted material. *The Feminine Mystique* rocked the earth beneath me. To defend my existence, to make worthy the ways I had chosen to live, I wrote "A Critique on the Mystique" as my personal rebuttal and looked to its pages for confirmation—which was not there—of the rightness of me as the woman I had become. Nothing I had done independently could be held in my hand or put on display. I had not spoken my truth. I had not, for years, opened my mouth by myself. Of all the things I had not done, the most important was to gain a skill, to protect myself and my children against poverty. I had worked, had sex, and married, in large part, for money. Not all women were bought before equal opportunity, but only a few were not.

For women, the years between Simone de Beauvoir's vision in *The Second Sex* and Friedan's call for action had seen a restlessness that systematically, somatically, struck at middle-class females. The pot was boiling. We had long waited to express ourselves. The eruption in the 1960s and 1970s was felt in every home in this nation and was celebrated or denied by all women. The time had come to storm the palace. Otherwise, we might never find the rest of what we were. We would grow old weeping.

The rebellion began in most women at about the same time, no matter how good things were for some of us. The women's movement set forth the urgent, critical need in us to substitute one kind of work for another, to have a name for the new work so that it could be announced or researched or simply included somewhere. Freud was wrong about the source of hysteria in women—it does come from sexual abuse —but he was right, on the nose, about our needing both love and work. In the 1960s and 1970s, women all over the country were looking for something to do that would blow up their balloons. I had lugged around airless balloons from the time of my father's suicide.

An invisible line was drawn within the population of women that divided women who were traditional and hid their anger, from women who were openly angry, an unpopular lot, loud and unpretty. The quiet women secretly hoped that the militant women would make change for everyone, which is what happened. I marched, funded, organized, and lived the movement every moment of the day and most of the night. I became even more of an outsider but, unlike Colin Wilson's original outsider, I did not want to get in. All I wanted to do was to get free.

On yet another sunny Saint Patrick's Day, two dozen women came to my house for dinner, and one by one we stood up and talked about our thoughts and feelings and dreams. We exchanged ourselves with each other. In the land of narcissism and phoney, on Chadbourne Avenue in Brentwood, there was a true opening of women's hearts that joined with the openings of other women's hearts in other cities and formed a foundation and structure for the feminist movement. Sisterhood was its soul.

At first, we did not know that women talking to women would become a force so powerful that it would change our society and affect the world. As contentious as many feminists were, as ridiculous and ludicrous as some of our dreams were, as absurdly as some of us behaved, the women I worked beside in the movement were cut from strong, enduring cloth. The underpinnings of the history I have lived gained women personal freedom, a term of utmost meaning to all of us and one that only we can define.

California was not in the women's movement, according to its history as written by New York journalists, but some of the great feminists lived in Los Angeles and San Francisco. They held up one side of the nation and made changes in the law of the land. (There is a lovely message hidden in these accomplishments. It may take millions of dollars to elect a state or national official, but it took only beans for women to change the mind-set of people around the world.)

I was wounded during the years of the women's movement, as were many women. We went from life as it was, through a wrenching change into life in its new form. Some women escaped the interim phase and died quickly. Others stayed where they were and took some light into the darkened rooms where they and their mothers lived. Daughters and grandchildren of the first modern-day feminists, who did not want to be the second sex any longer, are genetically arranged according to the words written in *The Second Sex* by de Beauvoir. In a macro sense, that is the story of women in the twentieth century; in micro, it is my story.

ROSLYN SOBEL

A TRAILER PARK in Newport Beach was our home in the summers when my daughters were little. We rented a one-and-a-half-bedroom mobile home that was anchored in the ground, and I sat with other women on the beach and watched our children as they played in the sand and swam in the bay. The men came down on the weekends from the cities nearby. Roz and her daughter visited us regularly and, while the girls played together, she and I would play cards and anything else we could find that was competitive. Word games were the most fun, but we put a special twist on double solitaire that made it last for hours and always had us roaring with laughter, side-splitting, crying, shrieking laughter that only Roz could give me. Her own laugh would shake clouds from the sky.

Heroic in her person, Roz lived a story of unfulfillment that was ordinary, common to many women of her time. Roz's husband was a musician, mine was a writer. Our lives were different but our roles were much the same: prototypes in a culture needing to be changed. We were not alike. She was gentler, more knowledgeable. We were confidantes, debaters, allies. We gossiped. We solved national and international crises and made inroads into the problems of the universe.

Roz was as graceful as a high-stepping chorus line, as charming as the Lunts, as intelligent as anyone I have ever known. I adored her. Everyone did. Men fell in love with her. Roz was not pretty but she was seductive, not beautiful but magical and alluring. Each one of her women friends felt that she was Roz's best friend. Roz made everyone she loved feel specially loved, somehow different from the way she loved other people.

I have always believed that it was Roz's mother who caused the tragedy that Roz held in her gut and that became cancerous. Some fathers and mothers, like my mother and Roz's mother, and the mothers or fathers of many men and women I have known, ill-treat their kids, damaging them for life or even killing some of them, like Roz, who seemed to have been made with weaker tissue than most. Weak tissue is all, sometimes, one needs to know to understand another person, or even oneself.

My friend's suffering from cancer became unbearable. Death was appropriate, but the right to die had not yet been tested in the courts. Roz's exitline was too long. For months and weeks and days we watched her enter consciousness for hours, then minutes, then seconds. We all mourned her before she died, but none of us was prepared for the pain we felt when we lost her. In the late afternoon, during the downward daily trek of the California sun, she raised her skeletal body up in bed, looked at me, smiled, and spoke my name. It was the last time I heard her speak.

When Roz died, the loss to me was of the same magnitude as the death of my father, and there was a space in the world that could not be filled. No one played word games, or loved me, like Roz. She was the only person, man or woman, on earth or in heaven or hell, who never hurt me, not with one word or one sentence, not in all the years of our friendship. She was incapable of betrayal; she had my complete trust. Roslyn Sobel and I gave each other unconditional love. She could have been my biological sister.

I wish she had been my sister.

MOST OF THE TALENT in Hollywood—writers, directors, actors—have poor business heads. They use agents to negotiate employment deals and they hire business managers to handle their money. Lawyers have complex functions as legal adviser/father/ financial overseer/lay therapist. Creative talent is the back on which the professional sector rides. Fair enough. Except when the lawyer/agent/business manager is a man like Dick W.

A whizbang with women, a black belt in selling clients to other clients and collecting from both, Dick W had a history that was at the least controversial. I left town before all of it was uncovered. He owned a building that housed attorneys, investment advisers, tax lawyers, real estate specialists, CPAs, and assorted tall corporate-type males who managed many many millions of dollars for some of the highest-paid talent in the business. Dick W himself was an attractive man with a multimillion-dollar smile. He smiled when you met him, he smiled when he went over your finances with you, he smiled when your money went down the tubes.

The poor judgment and tax-avoidance schemes of

Hollywood business managers were well known to us when we were Dick W's smallest account. He had put us in tax shelters, a prevalent economic strategy in the 1970s, and though they reduced our tax bill, we were required to make huge and risky investments in a variety of partnerships that kept us illiquid for many years. We owned portions of a dozen or more properties. One or two of them were good; the rest, with Dick W smiling, became worthless. An attorney friend told us to pay our taxes, to forget shelters. "It's cleaner and easier and cheaper in the long run," advised Deane Johnson.

Dick W, who had put together shelters for all his clients, disagreed.

Weary of being controlled by business managers and paying astronomical bills for advice that always resulted in our losing money, Norman and I agreed that I would be responsible for the finances of our family. I read books for a year. I learned about money as best I could, finding a haven of clarity and warmth and basic information in Harry Browne's books, such as *How You Can Profit from the Coming Revaluation*. Most economics texts were beyond me. I learned about current trends from periodicals.

We planned to make the change in two steps. The idea was to pass the control of our personal finances from Norman to me, at first under the supervision of Dick's office. Second, we would find a financial adviser more to our liking. The announcement of the first step was planned for one of our regular meetings with our CPA, real estate specialist, account manager, tax attorney, and Dick W himself present.

At the beginning of the meeting, Norman got up from the huge highly polished conference table and walked to my chair. Standing behind me, he delivered one sentence: "Frances will be working with you from now on."

He walked back to his seat and sat down. The conversation about our current portfolio began. All the remarks were directed to Norman. No one looked at me. Norman rose again, came back again to my chair, stood behind me, and repeated what he had said: "Frances will be working with you from now on."

After he was seated, the conversation took up where it had been interrupted, about the good shape our finances were in, plans for the next quarter, a full report by each man in the room, who looked at, spoke to, and smiled directly at Norman. No one looked at, spoke to, or smiled at me. Norman, a man who does not take the ignoring of his edicts well, made a third pass at the group, this time with some considerable annoyance, his message clear to anyone who was conscious. Nothing changed.

The next morning, after making further plans for handling our finances, plans that included Deane Johnson and a splendid tax attorney in his firm, I called up Dick W.

"Hello, Dick?"

"Yes, this is Dick." I could hear his smile.

"Dick, this is Frances Lear."

"Oh, hello, Frances," said he, still smiling. "How are you?"

"I'm just fine, Dick."

"Good; what's up?"

"You're fired."

I was certain that my remark would not have wiped the smile off his face even if we had been in the same room. No, he would have looked straight at me, still smiling, and tried to oil his way back into my good graces and regain our account. I do not kid myself into thinking that Dick W changed his attitude toward women because of me, and Norman and I are still climbing out of tax shelters, but my personal victory was sweet. Norman and I won it together, the way it should be.

WILLIE MAE ISHMON

SHE WAS MY CHILDREN'S "NANNY" and my friend through my years of terrible depressions and highs and a troubled marriage. She was as dependable as the sun and made the best chocolate pie in the history of the genre, and was forever smiling or laughing with her gold tooth showing and her great body shaking and her giggle that should have come out of a child. Willie's big problem, like mine, was men.

My first real family home in California was a tract house on a cul-de-sac in Encino. A large barren hill at the end of our backyard leaked muddy water whenever it rained. I stayed home with my children, but, when they were old enough to go to school, Willie and I were alone in the house all day. Both of us had been in interesting and tumultuous affairs and marriages. Willie wore a gold heart from one of her men in the middle of her chest, halfway between her neck and her great caramel-colored breasts; but she never loved a good man, only the ones who were content to live off her and stay in bed until she came home, eating her food and drinking the whiskey she paid for.

"Willie Mae." I was stern. "Get rid of him."

"I will," she promised.

But she did not get rid of him until there was another man ready to lie in her bed, eat her food, and drink her whiskey.

That upbeat, hip, tender, sweet, generous woman knew everything about personal politics. She stood in the middle of our family, between the fighting factions, as my Nanny had done with my mother and me, flashing her gold tooth, fists dug into her mammoth waist, eyes leveled at one of us, scolding in a manner that somehow caressed and held love. We rewarded her for ending the conflict by surprising her the next day with an orange gift. Willie loved orange more than diamonds or gold. The doors in her apartment were painted orange, and there was a huge orange cloth chair with a dark metal frame, orange lamps and rugs and ashtrays and plastic picture frames. She would have lived in an all-orange house down to the plumbing if it had been available. Willie was the color orange, in her home and in her self.

Before Kate was born, Willie came to us only once a week. As the years went by, there were bigger houses and more work and far less of me. I hated housework, and my depressions returned frequently and became increasingly severe. Willie began coming two, then three, then five days a week, but she would never "live in." She had to go home each night to her man and party with him and come back in the morning and complain, as I would, about men.

I trusted Willie with my children and with Ellen, Norman's older daughter who lived with us, and I trusted her to take care of me when I was in darkness, and I laughed with her and my children and their father for years and years before she began to cough up blood. Willie knew she had cancer and that she would die, but the knowledge that life would be taken from her in a very short time did not frighten her. When her gut hurt so much that she could not work, she let us take her to the doctor.

"Willie, you're not scared, are you?"

"Why should I be? I'm going to heaven. It's a mighty fine place."

I guessed that Willie saw a great kingdom up in the sky. "What does heaven look like?"

I had never known a fundamentalist Christian before Willie. Her description of heaven—she allowed it pink clouds; the rest was orange—was extravagant, blissful, sparkling, and filled with gorgeous men. There would be good men there for her to love. She would ride in a horse-drawn carriage and lie upon a cloud and play with the angels and laugh at their jokes and smoke orange cigarettes. The largess of the Lord would give Willie her land of milk and honey as contrast to her life, I supposed.

But that was not why Willie believed in heaven.

Not at all. I had the wrong slant, and I wish I could tell her so now. Willie was quite content with her life, she did not fight the cancer, she loved all her men, she had enough to live on, and she dearly loved being with us. Willie's heaven had all measure of things that were wondrous in themselves, not in comparison to anything on earth. Even happiness was not the same; it was constant and everywhere.

I picked a rose from the blanket we had ordered for her casket and placed it in the crook of her arm, beneath her great breast, adjacent to her heart, as if the five of us were that rose, as if it would live beside her as she lay upon her cloud and loved her man and smiled with her gold tooth showing.

SEX AS PRACTICED outside the home by married men in Hollywood has nothing to do with fidelity or infidelity or the amount of love and respect a man has for his wife. Sex is about supply and demand in Hollywood. There is only supply. A man has to be agile to avoid it, especially if he is an executive or a director who casts actors in television and films. Sex as practiced by most young hopefuls is, in their minds, part of the package to stardom. This is a bitch of a belief system to live with if you are married to someone in the business. Any woman who does not know that her husband is—with few exceptions—unfaithful to her will, in time, find out that he is. One way of learning this is by getting an I-fuck-your-husband look from an actress.

The Hollywood husbands who fool around successfully, who keep their affairs hidden, who are widely reputed to be faithful, portray themselves, carefully, with great skill, as family men.

"Only two men in this town are faithful to their wives," said a young woman director, confiding their names to me. She was wrong about both men, but they were tough calls. The men's role-playing was perfect, even when their lovers were in the same room with their wives, or when the men were talking to both spouse and mistress at the same time. The wife of a successful husband has, sometimes unknowingly, socialized at industry functions with a number of his afternoon lays. Most wives have become wise to this scene and bury the knowledge in the dark corners of their heads. Extramarital sex in Hollywood is an intricate and tightly woven web that gets thicker and heavier with each wedding anniversary.

Intelligent women in Hollywood who have been married for a long time do not leave their husbands upon the discovery of an affair. They have genuine love for their men, and most women have seen the pain and loneliness of divorce in the lives of their friends. My friend Grace H had been married thirty-two years when her husband, weary of guilt and bored with his mistress, announced to her that he had been having an affair with his secretary for years. Grace's husband is one of the family-man fictions. They produce the most tender of cuckolded wives, women who are least able to recover from the cracking of the icon. The wives, too, have bought into the image.

Grace H came from her house in Beverly Hills to mine in Brentwood every day for two months while she resolved what she should have worked out thirty years before. It is easier to accept infidelity as a part of the culture when your breasts tilt upward. At

Grace's age, there was always the fear that her husband had gone from her bed forever, or that this affair would end and another begin, that all the learning to forgive, even the attempt to forget, would not stop him from having the next affair and the one after that. Grace's fear was real and remained permanent, written into the script that Hollywood acts out.

I know of one very special marriage that broke apart for ten years while the husband had an affair with an unattractive, promiscuous, but bright and sexy woman. After the initial shock shattered the wife's heart, she did nothing. Patiently, quietly, her tears hidden from all but me, she held tight her knowledge that he would come back to her. I have never seen such faith and love, as well as fear and self-doubt, and I marvel now, many years later, at this woman—there must be others whom I do not know —who rewrote the script by herself: no director, no producer, no cast, and no crew; just one woman in love with one man she believed would come home. And he did. They are happy and inseparable and old. In Hollywood, where there is a superabundance of remarkable young flesh, where the youth culture will prevail until hell freezes over, one takes faithfulness whenever it is offered. It may not come around again.

MANIC-DEPRESSIVE
ILLNESS

BEFORE I WENT on lithium in my fiftieth year, whenever I was on a manic high, a chemical high, I would sit down at the typewriter without a clear thought but with a direction, and the pages would come out finished, written not by me but by me on the moon, by another, literally a different, self.

Writing is much more difficult for me now. Lithium cuts off the highs and levels them almost to the ground, like bulldozers lop off mountaintops. I am without the magic, the ability that came from nowhere human, and I sit and wrench out the work. Many people believe that manic-depressive illness is merely a romanticized excuse for being difficult. That is not true. In addition to the presence of a chemical imbalance, there is an unexplained factor in the illness that gives us an outsized possibility of doing good work.

I do not have a true gift for words, like one friend who writes with God in his pen, nor could my work touch the hem of literature. But when I am writing in a manic high, I have something many writers do not have. It is worth no more than the fact of itself and does not figure in the sum and substance of the written word, but every moment is rare and exquisite for me: I feel I am in the company of the greats. One person with manic-depressive illness understands what another person with the illness feels when he or she is working.

As a patient, I have described, countless numbers of times, to all the doctors who have treated me, the particular pain that comes in a depression. The details of my story are the same each time, with the same intensity, the same hopelessness, but something was always missing in the communication. I could not catch the link that was not there between us. Did they not understand when I said that I felt the pain *in my soul*? It is different from physical pain and is not knowable to someone who has not felt it.

Dr. R has patients with manic-depressive illness who explain their suffering to him. He went into a depression himself for the first time in his life while I was seeing him. He asked, "Why didn't you tell me there was actual pain in depression?" I thought I had made it clear many times.

With the discoveries of modern genetic engineering, some members of the medical profession question us as to whether or not we would give up our flawed genes and be without our illnesses. An interesting quandary. No one suffers more than the mentally ill, yet most of us have told our questioners that, given the choice, we would not give it up. One friend said she hoped her children would inherit her gene now that there are drugs to control the mood swings and the suffering.

A mood swing starts with a high and, by its nature, depression must follow, since a mood swing is much like the U.S. Postal Service or the earth itself. The cocksucker has to go through its "appointed rounds."

RITUALS

BETWEEN THE MANIA and the darkness that followed, I was a trolley car, a shrill, clanging, weather-beaten, worn, and ancient vehicle that ricocheted off the curbs as it sped along its customary route before crashing. Upon impact, nothing remained as it was. Lamed, unreasoning, the trolley car that was me had entered another depression, marked by the replaying of a ritual, one of many repeat performances, similar in content when the man was the same, different with different men, aimed at the soft pate in his self. Sophisticated, clever, hurtful button-pushing was my intent.

The point was to send him away after he had retaliated and angered me and then, with my miraculous, powerful, loving self, make him return. The ritual was to raise Lazarus from the dead, or bring Herb Loeb back. The theme of loss began the play, carved into my self with chisels and hammers and endless rows of sharpened tools. I learned from two fathers who split and one who molested me, from Bob Goodman, and, when I became a woman, from Sidney Fast, that the men I love will be lost, that I must have the power to bring them back and must keep that power exercised, in shape, at the ready, just in case, in the event of a sudden bursting blood vessel or a plane crash or the simple act of walking out the door. Endings can be avoided, lost articles of love can be returned, fate can be rerouted. It was a matter of my life or death.

The men I loved knew when the ritual was coming. The wonder was that, despite the warning, remembering, as they must have remembered, all the previous rituals, the other scenes of low blows and rage and intolerable unkindness, none of them ran beyond my reach. The scenario cannot be Xeroxed nor can it be recalled exactly as it was written, but the gist of it, the spilling out of anger toward men, the deepest sink into self-pity, the giving of well-oiled lies, the slashing of my target's self-esteem, would make an onlooker think that in this hour of raw sensibility, as one head of Hydra, I wanted to lop off the guy's dick. Not true. All I wanted was to be listened to in a serious fashion, to make him, all the hims, understand that to me a hurt was not a hurt; it was a lethal blow.

My rituals were high theater, but after each one came breathing space before the next monthly depression took control of me, when I was not high or down; nor did I, for that blessed time, fear loss. There were days and weeks in between the mood swings when I was out of danger. For the length of those times, I lay down with someone who soothed me and loved me and healed me. I was, then, a person to love.

CHARISMA

ALINE HAD CHARISMA. My father did not. Movie
stars have charisma, as do some politicians and most
saints. Cronkite and Cosby have—Callas and Chanel
had—charisma, among people whose names start
with C. Big Industry Names in all industries are believed to have charisma even if they don't; the same
holds true for presidents. Charisma has a great deal
to do with energy, which is connected to the electric-
ity in our bodies and is the product of our biological
chemistry. But, of course, we know that body chemistry is seriously affected by our psychology.

The people I know personally who produce excitement in a room—people who can keep an audience enraptured—have differing amounts of energy
and are quite diverse in their personality "type." But
these folk have one thing in common: a big black hole
in the center of themselves that must be filled up.
Much of their lives has been spent in developing the
skill of getting attention, which is the antidote to the
emptiness within. The size of the hole is, on the
average, in the estimation of one lay mind and without means of accurate measurement, directly pro-
portional to the hole owner's charisma. Charisma is

often a magical defense against the black hole showing.

A great many people have black holes but lack charisma, and there are people whose chemistry is awry, who may or may not have a hole of significance but are charismatic. Not-quite-right chemistry can be, in itself, the generator of a special electrical power. Men and women with manic-depressive illness can walk into a room and spread excitement, particularly when they are hypomanic, on a high. Or in an instant, when they are down, they can shove everybody around them into a stupor. Therefore, people with odd chemistry, and a well-developed sense of nonbeing, can be the most charismatic people in town.

I HAVE BEEN in therapy since I was thirteen years old, and much of it was bad for my health. The labors of most of my therapists bled into each other like batik-dyed cloth, one series of treatments indistinguishable from another—always with the second-best psychiatrist, who was recommended by the best psychiatrist, who was too busy to see me or too fearful of failure with manic-depressive illness—digging up and labeling and hammering out the patterns of my life at $30, $60, $100, $200 an hour.

The worst of them was Dr. G, who convinced the patients he found attractive that their health depended upon having sex with him. Common practice. He gave me a few shots of whiskey at the beginning of each session, had me undress in front of him and go through the session naked. We had intercourse once. I never understood why once was enough for him, but I am grateful that he was disappointed in me, or easily satisfied.

Dr. M worked in a spare, colorless Westwood basement office. His records of my treatment, if correctly annotated, would include (1) severe monthly mood swings (2) a serious suicide attempt (3) harmful mismedication. The final hour we spent together, when I announced that I was leaving California and ending my eight years of therapy with him, was a benchmark in my long experience with psychiatry.

"You'll be back in three years. Mark my words."

I am marking his words now, many years after the three years have passed. I am marking them, replaying them, remembering them, and they get no truer or more revealing of insight and competence than when he spoke them.

Trying to determine the stuff that separates good therapists from the chaff is irresistible though futile, so covered up are they in beige sweaters and eyeglasses and plain dark suits. A handful of therapists are artists. They have found something that works: a combination of humility, excellent knowledge, and an honest interest in helping the patient get well.

Other conclusions are inescapable. There is no fail-safe for a patient whose psychiatrist can be snookered. All but a handful of psychiatrists can be corrupted by fame; they hanker for it themselves. Good therapists are warmhearted and make good mates and good parents. No therapist should be allowed, under God's law or man's law or some law that has yet to be written, to have sex with his or her patient. Seductiveness in a psychiatrist may feel like a harbor in a storm, but it is a sure way to shipwreck.

When I was not in session with Dr. M, I worked with Dr. Russell Andrew, a clinical psychologist recommended to me by a friend. Or I lay in bed in my lovely home in Brentwood and fantasized another life in another place where I would do work that would bring me respect and reward. Or I would fantasize my death. I moved from my bed to one office or the other every day for years, wasting time with Dr. M, working hard with Dr. Andrew, invading the places in my heart that had pained me all my life.

Dr. Andrew carried me, dead weight, dependent, depressed, as if upon his back through the fifteen years it took me to leave my marriage. His skill, patience, and rare insight into the psychology of women kept me afloat in my present life while I tore away at the layers of my past. The events of my childhood (which Norman had described as Dickensian) had been recalled in other offices with other doctors and now with Dr. M three times a week, but Dr. Andrew connected them, in a way I understood, to the happenings and feelings I was experiencing in the present. He and I fought for my health, for dominance over my mood swings. His optimism about life influenced me to rethink my habit of ferreting out the dark side. He changed the direction of my life. His treatment gave me a tenuous, but real, hold on the reins of my moods.

One morning after leaving Dr. Andrew's office, I drove along Santa Monica Boulevard. Instead of getting off at Cliffwood Drive, my usual route home, I continued on absentmindedly in the direction of the beach. Dr. Andrew's words, my experiences both healthy and unhealthy, the potential of my life that I was ignoring, the relationships I was pushing to the edge, my deep fatigue from depression, the result of years spent probing into my past—all came together and produced a staggering moment of psychological revelation. The flash of insight is normal in therapy. One feels an immediate lightening of the heart. The spirit soars. The soul rejoices.

I stopped the car and walked across the sidewalk to a flowering bush and picked one of the blossoms and detached the petals one by one, folding them in half and the half into halves until they were tiny slivers. I bent down and put one of the folded petals into a crack in the sidewalk, pushing it into the open space until it could no longer be seen. I repeated the process with another petal, and then another, until all the petals were out of sight. The drive home was short. I pulled back the blackout drapes in my bedroom and let my life in with the light.

I had buried my past.

REHABILITATION

I ADMITTED I WAS an alcoholic in my sixty-first year, having hidden behind set phrases like "problem drinker," "allergic to alcohol," "addictive personality"; and when I was diagnosed as manic-depressive at fifty, the illness had become my excuse. Only Dr. Andrew among my therapists called my "problem drinking" by its right name, despite a history that went all the way back to blackouts during my teens, when I would get drunk in preparation for necking and petting. Blackouts allowed me to have feelings of love and belonging and erased my shame at being touched by a boy or a man who meant nothing to me. Blackouts and, later, pills and marijuana sheltered me from the sight of me.

I have stopped drinking with the help of AA, but the only substance I could not defeat under my own power, including Valium and other addictive medications, was marijuana, which I smoked in California for more than five years. My grass was the best in town. My connection serviced the industry. I doled out portions to friends but kept a stash for myself that would have turned on Australia.

Laguna Beach, second in rank to La Jolla, is the

tourist sleaze-art center of the Southern California coast. High atop a steeply inclined hill sits a modest institutional building, severe, white, cold. One suspects crazies live there. They do. Rehab, detox time, is the toughest, most mind-crushing process that one can go through. I would choose the pain of childbirth or pass kidney stones rather than withdraw from a substance. My AA sponsor had learned from me that I was smoking joints, drinking a bottle of wine every night, and in a paralyzing depression. She plugged into her network, found the center that was right for me, and made certain that someone accompanied me on the drive down. The attendants immediately put me into a small room, unfurnished except for a bed, and shot me full of something that put me away for two days. I was about to be washed clean and spun dry.

"I am not like them," I said to myself when I woke up. The halls and the dining room were filled with listless, hopeless, bedraggled men and women, slouched down in their chairs, scuffing their slippers on the floor, sullen, silent, most smoking cigarettes —an addiction I had overcome twenty years before. "I am addicted to grass, but I have conquered other substances, including alcohol. Surely I am healthier than these people."

Not true. I walked the floors most of the days and through long sleepless nights with men and women who were just like me, in the same amount of pain, struggling with lifelong deep-seated problems. The quiet empty aloneness of my room seemed intolerable. I asked to have a radio and was given permission to have one brought to me from home, along with some clothes and personal odds and ends. I listened to music from early morning throughout the night even when, if, I slept—country, pop, rock, classical. Music gave me proof of my existence. I was at least capable of receiving sound. Friends came to visit, which made me fearful. Addiction is repugnant to others, repugnant and embarrassing to me. My dear friend Betty Dorso sat with me beneath a huge small-leafed tree, and, because I was too sick to speak, we did not speak. In one hour, a small and precious time during those torturous days, Betty gave me a generous portion of her inner peace.

The task of recovery began both in group therapy and in one-on-one sessions. We retrained our bodies with exercise, and we dug into our minds with the help of biofeedback, relaxation tapes, and mandatory AA meetings. The measure of a good rehab center is whether it can turn an addict's head around in only six weeks. The probability of that is not good, but the odds improve when the therapist is talented. I lucked out. A young European, Lau Hanning, forced me to face my addiction, to understand the meaning of being an addict, and to accept the truth that addiction is permanent and requires lifelong vigilance.

The young people I met in the group therapy

sessions were heartbreaking, their minds closed off from the events in their lives that had wounded them, that had to be explored before there was hope of getting well. Their first task would be to overcome their image of themselves as victims. The very sick crouched in the corners; the rest of us made an imperfect circle around Hanning as he explained the unexplainable, the incomprehensible. My many years in therapy had opened up a space where his words could enter, but my demons were firmly in place. I looked at them daily but they would not budge.

"Why," asked Hanning in a private session, "are you still alive? There is every reason for you not to have survived."

An odd question but an effective one. Why was I alive? Why had I not given up long before?

"Because"—the answer came quickly, as if I had known it all my life—"because there is something I have to do."

Hanning was silent.

"I don't believe in fate or destiny. They are so grandiose, so all-powerful, but I do believe in the individual, and perhaps the something I have to do is, simply, my best. Since we never know what our best is, or whether we have already done it, or if it is still to be done, the challenge keeps inspiring me. I don't expect to be graded on my lifetime performance or handed a report card at the pearly gates. I need to please myself."

In my room alone, I listened to music and looked inside myself for answers and outside myself for reasons, back and forth from the past to the present, one against the other. In time, within the six weeks of rehab grace, I opted for the future. Psychodrama, a technique used in group therapy, loosened my stubborn residual hold upon mind-altering substances by revealing the true and painful feelings between another patient and his family.

The boy was not out of his twenties. His face was deeply sad, as were all the faces in the room, but his held an innocence unlike the older, hardened ones that watched him. His mother was pretty, plainly dressed, ten pounds overweight, traditional, Middle American, out of place in this West Coast facility for alcoholics and drug abusers. Her husband was the cut of man who inspired the rise of feminism. To him, his wife was the second sex and his son was "garbage." The word did not come out until the three of them had gotten into a raging fight, but when "garbage" was spoken, there was, as if recalled by a computer, a memory in each brain in that room that set in motion the pain of parental disdain.

The injuries received from unloving parents, the behavior of alcoholic families, the juxtaposition of mental illness and addiction, the known and unknown facts of substance abuse, are powerful, irrefutable reasons for victimization. Life is at its most pathetic in rehab, yet many of the patients are superior by far, more admirable, more worthy, more courageous, than the majority of their visitors.

The miracle of recovery, beyond science, beyond cause and effect, lies within the mystery of the life force and is likely centered in one's faith or in having an essential goal, be it just to stay alive. During the time I worked with Hanning and adhered to the center's strict and healing routine, I began the eventual taming of a demon I had been frightened to confront all my life. I came late to a wobbly but mounting inner security. I no longer had to hide.

FANTASY LIFE

FANTASY IN CHILDHOOD is a solution to an unsolvable problem.

Herb is sitting on the ceiling of my room after I come home from the Meiers', his handsome face drained of the unfamiliar pinkish color. My pleasure at seeing him is mixed with anger. More anger than pleasure.

"Why did you leave me? No matter what was wrong, it would have been better if we were together." I speak in a loud whisper.

My father is a silent man and does not answer, but I insist, needing to know the story. Weary of listening to my repeated questions, he gives in and then we talk. During the exchange, I have it out with him. He apologizes, putting the blame on my mother, who, he says, threatened to leave him and take me with her if he lost his money.

In the context of my suddenly full-fledged fantasy world, over which I was soon to discover I had total control, my father was telling me the truth. I kept Herb on the ceiling until I was older, when I stopped speaking to him and learned to satisfy my needs in my imagination by remaking, to my liking, the words and feelings that I received from other men and women. The distinction between fantasy and reality did not become important to me until late in life, when I found it necessary to put away childish things. I do not regret one moment that I have lived in fantasy, for there was nothing that I wanted that I did not have, nor any love left unrequited. I have made up conversations with everyone I liked or disliked or read about who interested me, and I put myself in bed with those I found attractive. I imagined myself being brilliant, standing on top of the world in sight of everyone. Sometimes I am the guest speaker behind a podium in a Jacqueline de Ribes gown. The hall is the largest I have ever seen.

I have lived my fantasies with, and placed my expectations in, men and women of great superiority and excellence. In my imaginings, they are without annoying habits and there is little weakness in their characters. I have endowed each one with admirable qualities. They make me laugh, they adore me, they are surprisingly malleable. There is no tedium in being in their company.

A man enters my life. His eyes promise a conduit to my father. He seems kind and interested in me, and so I visit the factory where I make fantasy and take a casual exchange between this unknown man and myself and make of it an acorn, a dab of color, a hint of plot, and churn out, again, once more, a great masterpiece of love and sex and companionship and laughter and a connection of deep, wide, permanent tissue. This dancing in my mind is greater than the sum of all the parts that are missing in me. The man disappoints me and goes away and comes around again with another face, another name. A parade of men has marched through my head, men with psyches I have wiped clean, who lead to all there is for me to want, to all the caring I need to give, to matter and thought that makes me whole.

I must stop trying to connect with fantasy, though it is far into my life to entirely replace an old, well-entrenched system with a new one, and the track is slippery from use between truth and the region where I control as far as I can see and feel. But it is urgent for me to accept that I have connected with men and women many times. They did not resemble the face I saw on my ceiling as a child, but they were, and are, greatly satisfying to me, and once in a while, sometimes, they move close to reality.

PAUL

PAUL WAS MY LOVER for twelve years. Paul was
not his name. In the wonderings of family and
friends, there was little doubt that I was having an
affair with someone during that time, but he might
as well have been handsome Irving Wapner, who
painted our house, for all anyone knew. I have never
revealed his identity. I never will.

We met on a Thursday. We were not introduced,
nor were we shoved together at a cocktail party or at
someone's pool. Our worlds were far apart. We
would never have met in a traditional way. No proper
formal introduction would have been possible in this
life. Meetings of this sort are struck by the kindness
of destiny.

I had an eleven o'clock appointment with an in-
ternist, or at the lab for a lithium level, or a dentist's
recall, or a bone man or foot man or breast man or
some man, some doctor who would send me a
souped-up bill for something that was nothing. When
Paul came into the elevator, I stood at attention, on
dress parade. He was a split hair less beautiful than
Charles Boyer when Boyer was young, Mediterranean beautiful like Gianni Agnelli when Agnelli was

young. I had picked up men before. I had chosen one here, one there, but this one with a head like a lion, with a body that could only belong to a jock, whose eyes did not look at mine, did not case my body, did not size up my breasts or invade my crotch—this one was obviously, without question, not available.

The elevator stopped on three. He got out. The doors closed. He was gone.

I had not had sex with a man in four years, and there was no triumph for me in replicas. I envied women who held real flesh inside them. Alone in my bathroom on the soft fur rug, I thought of myself as deprived, unlovely, not a woman. Without a man's body on, in, loving mine, I felt obscene, the frustrated manipulator of a Magic Wand.

I went up to my floor, stayed in the car, and pressed three.

A woman could not—this much I knew—get this man for the wanting. His iron-black hair was massed on his head, which he held high in the air, looking off somewhere, busy with splendid imaginings, with complex thoughts, unneedful of earthly sights. This man was the best person for sex I ever saw. I had not tooled myself out of reality.

He is standing outside the elevator doors, waiting for me. "I knew you would come." I say nothing. He rushes into the car, pushes me to the wall, shoves himself into me, explodes, drowns, then we drop to the floor, quiet together, in love and empty of want.

The doors opened on the third floor. He was not there.

I circled the floor.

Sexual chemistry is an instantaneous knowledge about another person's rhythm and intensity. I have passed men on the street and have known how sex with them would be. Yet I have been in bed with men and searched in every way I knew how for a chemistry that would never be there. I have loved men with mild chemistry and accepted it, others with much chemistry and enjoyed it. And there is another category of attraction—not only chemistry but including it—another coming together for which there is no name. It happened to me long ago on the corner of Fifty-seventh Street and Fifth Avenue in New York City and it happened in the elevator with Paul, and I shall remember, until I am wizened and ready to go, each fraction of a second's look into another human's sexual building blocks. Twice, I have seen in a stranger's eyes every millimeter of sexual space within him, all of his man-self, his libidinous territory, spread out for me. Considering the number of streets I have traveled, the public conveyances I have ridden, the number of public rooms in the countless buildings I have entered and exited, I have looked into thousands of men's eyes, but these two pairs were different. They were a journey's end; the big bang in the sky.

I returned to the lobby, called my doctor and canceled my appointment, found a planter with a ledge wide enough to sit on, and waited. There was time to plan my approach. One draws upon cheap novels and sitcoms for material at a time such as this. I did not read cheap novels. I watched Norman's shows, but none dealt with picking up a man. The wait was short, my opening remarks, barely rehearsed, were not clever enough, too bold. The lion's head was abreast of me, then past me, then almost gone, again. I hurried after with every erg I could muster, with the heat I took from the air around me, switched on.

"Would you buy me a drink?"

I read his look.

I saw you in the elevator looking at me and I can't wait to get my hands on you.

He took my arm, held it close, and we walked, without a word, to the Beverly Wilshire bar. We exchanged pleasantries for a half hour, checked into the

hotel, and stayed in bed until we had introduced ourselves to each other, this time in a traditional way. I
gave what I could of myself, of my passion, which
was free, of my body's eagerness, my ready heart,
but not of the depth of me, which was bound to
memory.

"I can't come."

"You will." He was not arrogant.

Paul and I made love for half a year before I had
my first orgasm. The hot liquid flowed from inside
me as I walked down streets or sat in restaurants or
recalled a moment of sex or simply existed. I was a
healthy ancient adolescent.

The moment that has no name comes to both man
and woman at the same time, as it came to Paul and
me that day when I had just turned fifty and he was
fifty-three.

NEW YORK
1985–

MY ROOTS ARE in New York. I had been misplaced in California for almost thirty years. For many months I flew here at regular intervals, practicing for the final trip. In the last years of our marriage, Norman and I had bought an apartment at the Ritz Tower on Fifty-seventh Street for both business and pleasure, combining four small hotel suites into an ungraceful, oddly proportioned duplex. Robert Graham's bronze sculptures of naked men and women covered the round structural columns in the living room. Dark-red wool couches were arranged in a semicircle in front of a huge curved silver television screen that was sunk into one wall, as if life starts and ends facing TV.

Half my life had been spent as the wife-of, an often and traditionally enviable position. My marriage ended in the back of a Lear 35 jet, leaving behind sweet and tumultuous memories, dear friends, and the world I had lived in throughout my children's lives.

I moved to New York, taking very little with me —no husband-and-wife pictures, no mementos from the house, only the books and clothes I liked, none of the gowns I had worn to award dinners, nothing with sentiment—killing my past life by leaving it behind, as I had once killed my childhood by burying it in a broken Santa Monica sidewalk.

One life was lost. Would I find another?

My daughters had moved to New York years before and now lived in nearby apartments. Three long-time women friends were attentive and concerned. There was love to be had in New York, but separation and depression live together in me, so I withdrew from the world. Dr. Andrew carried me with his voice over the phone into the next hour, the next day. My daughters and my friends pierced the solid blackness around me for short periods, but depression seeks its own level and will not be seduced up. I was headed straight for the next overdose of pills and drink.

Unseen, the size of a germ, nothing I had packed, the most valuable possession I owned, the entrance to my next life, was stirring in the right side of my brain. I remembered a conversation between Norman Lear and Jim Autry, retired president of Meredith Magazines. Norman had just bought a trade publication.

"What makes a magazine great?" Norman asked Jim.

He answered, "Its mind-set."

A question from me: "What is a mind-set in a magazine?"

"*Vogue*'s is fashion. *Rolling Stone*'s is music."

"Where is my magazine?" I asked. When I travel, I buy only newsmagazines. Women's magazines are not targeted to me.

"No publisher in any of the publishing houses in New York has your mind-set."

A million tiny metal filings rearranged themselves around a magnet in me. In a quick summing-up of my collective experience with women, with writing, with fashion, with contemporary history, I knew I had the mind-set. I would do a magazine in New York. Work is the hard texture of me, my 911.

If I had been rational during the agony of separation, if I had been on speaking terms with reality, I would not have believed I could successfully publish a magazine. I would not have been so close to psychosis and as far into the need to make something: the blessing of manic-depressive illness.

CREDIBILITY

I HAVE ALWAYS aspired to something out of the ordinary. CredibleFrances, inseparable words I covet, earned by long slices of time learning the craft of putting things together in a stylish way.

My unknown origins, when considered in the extreme, when accompanied with my lost-identity disease, fed the recurring fear that I did not exist. How, then, to gain access to others, to be acknowledged by them and also by me? Credibility is made out of hard cold materials or proven supposings. Stepping-stones of theorem, invention, data. My credibility would be made of wet stucco, slapped onto myself, layer upon layer, trowel by trowel, until it was hardened into a house in which I would be certified, deeded, true.

So go ahead, said the voice in my head, swim the Pacific, jump from a plane and survive: do the magazine. Others had published magazines; I could. Herb's entrepreneurial gene could not have been passed on to me, but I am my father's daughter. I trusted the voice in my head, which does not fool around with me in the long term. Despite its sophomoric humor, it is always correct. This time, my gut and the voice agreed.

You will succeed, said the voice.

I will succeed, said me.

I could not be a journalist in the 1940s; I would be one in the 1980s. Was this magazine "something I had to do"? Would this project allow me to take my life and my self up from two on a scale of ten, to build my stucco house, to get out of bed in the daytime forever? Dr. Andrew's voice and my voice together brought life to the room where I hid and moved me, stirring up unused brain matter, tempting me, daring me with imaginings of good work, exciting me with visions of a product finished, tied up, sent out, done.

Introverted, depressed, naked of knowledge about magazines, scantily clothed in business affairs —I had lain awake all night when money was being transferred from California to New York; could the transaction get fouled up in the system?—I picked up the trowel, looked down at the wet moving mixture of portland cement, sand, and lime, and entered the most terrifying, exhilarating year of my life. The initial move from my bed to the word processor closed the door forever on the orphanage. Long miles stretched out ahead with no arrival point, but, in the place where there was not me, gray-colored matter was forming, not yet adhering, not yet a mass.

People came to lunch and I learned from them. They were the masters and I was the one who could afford to start a magazine. My divorce settlement was very large.

"You're living your own dream," said an able woman who dreamed of her own, though unattainable, dream of launching a magazine.

I was not a dream; not mine, not anyone's. I was the owner of an idea that everyone said was a good idea but one I could not execute. Why not? asked Dr. Andrew. The voice was still. I had to listen to me. Listening to me, hearing me, was a new form of communication. I had only reacted, emoted, felt. Gaining knowledge had never been a deliberate action for me. Now I wrote down what the masters said while they wondered about this woman from Hollywood who knew nothing about magazines. They came and ate salads and I asked them what a magazine was and they told me. Some of the masters taught me editorial; others taught me demographics, which I promptly forgot. No one told me of the terror, the panic of holding the project together up in the air all day and all night so it would not fall and break apart, the shame at the thought of failure, and the competition, the knowledge that, as one cute publishing executive said, "We'll cover you up at the newsstand." The idea required collaboration with people, with others' eyes, others' ears, with yeses and that's goods and noes, with do it over, with the fun of working in a team. For a long period I did not have a full team. But I had some expert help. Sixteen-hour days and seven-day weeks, mistake upon error, progress, growth, faltering, and we turned out a magazine that we named LEAR's. We had tried other names, but since there had been a Mr. McCall and a Mr. Forbes and a Mr. Harper, why not a Ms. Lear?

I am not fraudulent, but sometimes I have asked people to do things I could not yet do myself. I have set goals for myself by writing them down for others. I am strengthened by LEAR's editorial philosophy. Once I was as insecure as the sand on the beach. Still an outsider, I am not a less-than.

People in the publishing industry meet to eat and make deals at The Four Seasons restaurant. I had lunch there one day in the Grill Room in the path of entering and exiting executives, agents, and talent. One by one, the Big Industry Names came to my table and shook my hand and congratulated me on the first issues of LEAR's.

That day I became a house.

DR. KAY JAMISON, who is my friend, wears flowered or glittering dresses all year. She has an enviable beauty that needs little tending. Part intellectual, part visionary, part warrior, she will remove the stigma from mental illness. Kay's mother reminds me of springtime now, in the winter of her life. Both women look at life, at their memories, as a kind of stereopticon of bright happy scenes, of good work, of the experience of love, of close friends, of promise. My memories were dark. No streaks of light as contrast. The distance between our perceptions of the past was as great as the distance between the ends of the earth.

There is not one piece missing from Kay or her mother, unlike me and most of the men I have loved, who are fractions. Some essential part is lost from each of us. When we love, we find in someone else the empty space that matches the one in ourselves. We see a mirror reflection and believe we can fill the space in the other and they, in turn, will fill it in us. Magic, if one is incomplete, is finding one's complement and then believing the missing fractions in both of us can be filled up. But it is never so. You can count by the setting of the sun the time it will take for the man—or woman—who wrought the miracle to pack up his bag of tricks and go home.

A subculture of reclusiveness harbors us. There is safety in being alone. We feel best when we work. There is comfort in the decent lives we have made for ourselves. As outsiders, we are inside only with ourselves and those we can trust. Some lovers. Some friends. Some family. We are peaceful with each other, having nothing to explain. We expect from each other only what we are able to give of ourselves.

All the books and articles and talk by the New York journalists who defined feminism for the nation as women's independence did not have enough insight into, did not ascribe sufficient importance to, the superiority of interdependence; or to the injuries that occur to young girls, the results of being traumatized, abused; or to the vulnerability of such women to replays of the past. Women like me wear stubborn resistant damage, though overcome it can—and must—be. I challenge other feminists to deny the unresolved need felt by many women who have been deprived of early loving, or have suffered betrayal. My feminism is as credible as anyone's, and I had been dependent upon a man's love and loving a man, since when? Since I was in the orphanage? Since my father committed suicide? Since I lost Bob Goodman?

Since my stepfather? Since time began? I would be better off dead, as Evelyn said, if I had lived the greater part of my life without a man to love.

After leaving California, after my divorce, after the unbearable depression, after months of working until midnight and going straight to my apartment, alone, exhausted, pulling down the blinds and crawling into bed and turning on the television and going to sleep at some early hour of the morning, after nearly going mad from the grief of loss—not from the loss of my marriage but from the fact of loss—I understood that my life, at least for the time being, depended upon finding a way out of investing everything in one man. I realized that the traditional relationship of marriage, or living with a man, or seeing only one man, loving only one man, was, for this time in my life, too great a risk. I could not survive loss again.

The idea of having more than one man in my life, at least for a while, was given to me by a friend, a sexually active, unmarried, celebrated woman who explained her life to me.

"I have a man for every reason."

Why not? I thought. Diversify your investments, Frances. As long as you don't betray anyone, as long as you tell the truth, as long as you do not manipulate. As long as you are able to make them, and you, happy.

I have dipped into a younger generation for play,

for fun. I take advice from a smart businessman who is closer to my age. I treasure an artist who mindfucks me and inspires me. I continue to have sex monogamously. The style of my life is serious business. One needs substitutes waiting in the wings, and there must be time for my work, for family, for friends.

In a rare and perfect fantasy, I am aboard Mariner III, *a long, sparkling-white yacht, built in the 1940s, which I once glimpsed motoring through the canals of Fort Lauderdale, Florida. Behind its teak-framed cabin doors, on its broad and open rear deck, and with its handsome white-uniformed crew,* Mariner III *is the perfect vehicle for traveling from my vision of life to Kay's, which I covet. I will live on this glorious yacht as she rolls gently on the sea, and I will taste the wind, and swim off the ladder in the secret coves of the Mediterranean. All my men will be on board. One will do sports all day long; one hates boats and paces the deck; one is an artist who works in his room; one is a control freak who runs the ship with the captain and cooks with the chef. I will continue to write. I will lighten the sight of my life, and I will separate myself from the pain of the past. I have no interest in the fine Bordeaux served every night that would black me out. I like the light shining on me.*

SUICIDE ATTEMPTS

I HAVE ATTEMPTED SUICIDE, to the best of my memory, three times with serious intent and three times with minimal interest in the outcome. If one is sane, attempting suicide is an excellent means—and this is the pith of it—for testing, not consciously, the strength of one's self-destructive versus one's life forces. I wonder how people who do not experiment with suicide take this measure of themselves. There is some real advantage in being pushed to feel the edges of one's self, to know the exact bulk of one's inner resource.

The majority opinion is that taking one's life— not being able to work out one's problems—is an act of cowardice. I know of two kinds of suicide. One is no-choice, in which case courage or cowardice plays no part at all. The second category is suicide that is opted for. Since the motivation for suicide can be either, I do not believe anyone can know which category applies in any one suicide, nor am I convinced that there is truly a difference between the two. If suicide is opted for it must weigh in with more courage than one that is no-choice, but since the act is the same, the state of mind might also be the same.

I ascribed strength and courage to my father's suicide since I needed to remember him as a giant of a man. My attempts are no-choice. I must end the pain. The act demands neither strength nor weakness; it is simply there for me to do, which explains the high rate of suicide among those of us with manic-depressive illness. The part played in keeping us alive by proper medication and by competent therapists has not been measured, but it is safe to conjecture that many who have died would have had normal life spans had they received the proper treatment. That includes Van Gogh.

It is interesting to me that I, having been absorbed with death and suicide all my life, have no more insight into its cowardice or bravery than I have into the meaning of $E = mc^2$. I am on surer ground evaluating the part that blame and guilt play in the minds of those left behind. Whether or not a suicide is botched, family and friends look for the cause. Who is at fault? Why did she or he do it? I believe that the need to find the reason behind the act and to place the guilt is, in some way, palliative to those who are mourning. Releasing anger, focusing emotion on the villain in this inexplicable act, detours grief into other, if unfathomable, channels.

Almost everybody takes suicide personally. It is true that something or someone acts as a trigger and sets off a reaction that causes the pain that leads to suicide. But a trigger is a trigger. A trigger is not responsibility, not fault, not cause. No man or woman or child is strong enough to will death to a person who does not want to die. There is never enough withholding of love, or unleashing of anger, that can take away life from anyone who is not looking for an exitline.

A no-choice suicide does not contain the slightest hint of seduction of death, nor a snip of an invitation. If death is opted for, there are circumstances that significantly contribute toward the suicide. But, alas, unfortunately, the assumption or placement of blame is always muddled and knotted and tied up with theories and explanations and reasons, which tumble out for all the world to manipulate. Light in this particular darkness may not illuminate the truth.

Suicide can grow on family trees. As a word, it appears in police reports, in headlines, in good and bad poetry, in fiction and journalistic accounts, in state law, and in the thoughts of men and women like myself for whom death is a subplot of life.

GETTING OUT

THE ACTUAL ENDING was a long time in coming.
I spent some of the months prior to the event remembering a good meal here and there, sukiyaki in Encino, chocolate bread pudding in New York, pea soup in Brentwood, and potato bread in Southampton. I remembered some fine lovemaking in my apartment in New York, in the rented one in Los Angeles, and on a stale and crumpled bed in the country.

I had worked well, but most of it was hidden in achievements that benefited others—beginning with Mr. Burke of B. Altman, where I stood on my feet eight hours a day, six days a week, for a salary that barely covered the rent for a closet called a room in a dismal hotel on Twenty-third Street, where I lived for several weeks after I left home. My pal Billy Engel sent me three dozen roses that took up most of the space and all of the oxygen.

Like most women who depend on their looks, I had an estimation of myself that was greatly limited to my face and figure until I began to lose them. My sexual viability and my age struggled with each other in my consciousness, much as my past fought my will to live.

I concluded that my failures were of my making. I did not blame myself for the tragedies of others—like Aline's cancer or the Korean War or the demise of department store retailing. I recalled the ends of loving that I had caused and the loves I had lost through the fault of others. There was no pleasure in remembering my stubborn resistance to capping my temperament, my idiotic insistence upon holding all pain dear and close.

Suicide, for people like me who are enamored of it, who find life in death not the other way around, is another solution to an unanswerable question begun in childhood. Death, for some of us, is life without pain. The need to "repeat the trauma" (psychobabble) is like the electric prod that moves cattle, against which no beast or human can win. My obsession with death is my electric prod, which insinuates itself into my thoughts, causing a steady and fundamental decay. It also seems to act as a cover for its opposite. Since I am so hot for death, I am clearly terrified of life. So be it.

It is a bitch to commit suicide. There are never enough pills to be certain there should not be one more. That is the nightmare. Botching it. One too few pills; not leaving enough time before someone playing the hero rescues me; or my stomach rejecting the pills, the pinks first, the yellows next, and filling up again with the pain I have almost but not quite escaped.

When the time comes for the bedroom shade to be lowered and the yogurt and its spoon placed on the bedside table with the lithium tablets and the Klonopin, there is nothing left in the universe of my consciousness except the fear of botching it.

When the logistics have been worked out and the potion has kicked in, I will go back to the amazing light and the profound serenity I felt when I attempted suicide ten years ago and botched it, when I was close enough to death to know that the entrance to it is, indeed, heavenly. There is the absence of pain and a state of true peacefulness, so getting out is going to be a good experience for me.

Over my lifetime, I have built the place where I am going. Nothing is there. All is absent. There are no acorns or dabs of color or tissue. No light. Nothing is done there. Time does not run. The place has no center. I am in nothing and I am safe. Nothing reaches me. I see nothing. I hear nothing. The pain has slipped away from its usual berth in my soul. There is cause for joy but I do not feel joyous. As I predicted, I feel serene.

I am going to a place that holds out the most possibility for me. One takes off one's psyche there. The sacred and profane connection between me and my lifelong pain of lost parental love will be cut as I enter. I shall be able to do good work, for I believe that emotional unrest interferes with work, that the best one can do is done with a free mind.

The days will be warm and I will sit by the sea and write a book about something other than myself, and in the afternoons I will lie in the arms of a longtime lover who will make a truth of permanence.

GRAY

IN A DREAM I flip myself, as one would a coin, to see whether or not I will live. I am part nurse in all white, part patient trapped in an iron lung. My illness was old; iron lungs were the subject of movies and books forty years ago. My health is pristine, like my father's uniforms. Why am I still a debate, a split infinity? I have just come from the darkest black; next week I will be absent of color. I yearn for a muted middle gray to bring stability to the rest of my life.

Vermont. The day was still. The clouds remained in one design. The house was very old. The living room ceiling sagged in the middle. The kitchen was made of plywood—it had been converted from a greenhouse—and had cheap appliances, some jelly jars, battered pots and pans, stick-figure furniture. The grounds were brilliant. The yellow woods where Robert Frost had found his path were hidden behind a solid row of silver birch. The slope of ground from the side porch down to the road was covered with child-high weeds. The great stone fireplace could warm the entire state in midwinter.

Norman and I bought the house and tore it down and destroyed a national monument, and built a large country home that pleased every eye and filled every heart that entered it. My marriage was breaking apart, and I was seldom out of depression, but I loved Vermont. I felt nested there. We took long walks in the forest and along the roads and picked the wildflowers, which died before we got home. There was a real gala when everyone gathered for Christmas. The tree was splendid with ornaments we had collected for twenty years. We opened our gifts all day, there were so many. My whole life was in that house at one time, as was the pain of imminent inexorable separation.

Vermont was gray.

Southampton is at its best in the early spring. The greenery is broken by patches of reddish brown that will bloom later in the season. The yellow-and-white daffodils come up first, in bunches. Timothy has bordered them with rows of cone-shaped purple grape hyacinths. Here and there a bush is covered with blossoms. The beach is combed. By afternoon it will be broken by tire tracks and the footprints of the few people who walk along the water's edge. When there is a storm, the sea crashes against the beach in a rhythm that is perfect for sleeping. At other times, the sea laps gently against the shore, so still that I cannot hear a sound from my bedroom window just yards from the beach.

I come here all year. In winter the garden is stark naked. The autumn yellows and reds move to the fireplace, which burns all day and for hours into the night. The summer is my least favorite time anywhere, including the beach, but more people are in the house and that pleases me. The aesthetics of this house are most satisfying to me. The floors are painted celadon, the color of the sea at sunset. Every room is furnished minimally with tiny-striped fabrics and, on good days, they are filled with light and sun and fresh sea air.

Again July has come, the fourteenth of the month. My birthday is revisited. Each bed holds a sleeping family or extended family member. Two are flesh and blood, the others have gone the distance with me and are loyal and loving. The trees are spun with tiny white lights, and the fish is moist and tender. The ocean breeze blows out the candles on the cake my daughters have set down before me. We relight the candles quickly, and I blow them out to the last one. I am superstitious about candles on birthday cakes. I make the same wish again this year, and it is not to be bandied about by an indifferent whiff of air. My wish is always to be free. I wish each year to be free, but I do not know what it is I wish to be free of, or what has the power to keep me from being free. Do I choose to be tied to something? to what? why?

I have fucked up, made an ass of myself, lost control, lashed out, gone home, gotten into bed, taken a Serax, and slid into pain; my safety net, my wafer and wine. But I have held on to my sides for fear that they would break from laughing, have gotten another better job the next day every time I was fired, have held my children close, and I have held some good men. The better part of my life has been snake eyes, but I have won at every crap table I visited. I have failed to sit midway on the seesaw in this incarnation, but I have been in a larger air more often and higher than most.

In every life there are misthoughts, words remembered incorrectly, clichés that were not true. One such is the ordinary everyday misconception that we can rid ourselves of demons. We cannot. Demons, once formed, remain demons and do not become pure white swans or fields of golden wheat. Demons are evil. Demons are hell. They are born from being done to and grow to be habits that destroy. But demons are not of nature's making and can be mastered. The idea is to pin the suckers to the wall.

The voice in my head agreed.

"Girl"—the voice is pre-feminism—"enough with death and illness. Blacks and whites are pigments of your imagination." Punning is not unusual. "Mix the cans of paint yourself. Choose a shade of gray that warms and pleases you. Life is gray, but you have accepted neither life nor compromise. Your chemistry has protected you from living the truth. Get smart. Dump the mood swings. You have the new red pill and the old pink one and they work. Get your life together. Get off the stage. Bring the curtain down. Fade to black. Close the play. Drop the series. Write something new. Open with Act I, Scene I. Make it a musical."

A Note on the Type

This book was set in Garamond, a typeface originally designed by the famous Parisian type cutter Claude Garamond (1480–1561). This version of Garamond was modeled on a 1592 specimen sheet from the Egenolff-Berner foundry, which was produced from types thought to have been brought to Frankfurt by Jacques Sabon (d. 1580).

Claude Garamond is one of the most famous type designers in printing history. His distinguished romans and italics first appeared in Opera Ciceronis *in 1543–44. While delightfully unconventional in design, the Garamond types are clear and open, yet maintain an elegance and precision of line that mark them as French.*

Composed by Dix Type, Syracuse, New York

Printed and bound by Arcata Graphics, Martinsburg, West Virginia

Designed by Iris Weinstein